TEACHING

OFF THE WALL

BULLETIN BOARDS IN ACTION

ELAINE PRIZZI
JEANNE HOFFMAN

Fearon Teacher Aids
Carthage, Illinois

Editorial director: Roberta Suid

Designer: Paul Quin & Associates

Copyright © 1981 by Fearon Teacher Aids, 1204 Buchanan Street,
P.O. Box 280, Carthage, Illinois 62321. All rights reserved. No part of this
book may be reproduced by any means, transmitted, or translated into a
machine language without written permission from the publisher.

ISBN–0–8224–6830–1

Library of Congress Catalog Card Number: 80–81836

Printed in the United States of America.

CONTENTS

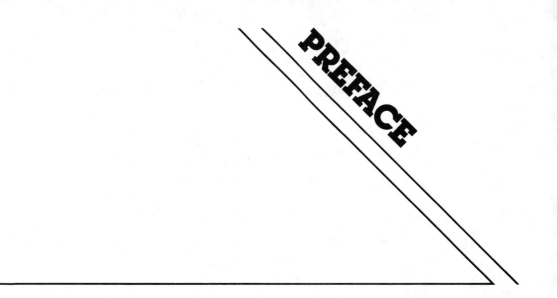

PREFACE

Do you sometimes feel like a classroom decorator? Do you spend hours preparing a clever bulletin board only to have your ingenious eye-catcher treated like just another wall covering? If so, now is the time to change your pattern of bulletin board thinking.

You can turn your classroom "wall coverings" into important tools in the learning process. Your time can be used in constructing bulletin boards that attract attention *and* have teaching objectives.

The goal of *Teaching Off the Wall* is to provide teachers and classroom aides with the techniques for putting bulletin boards into action.

- Chapter 1 describes the *active approach* to bulletin board construction and shows how you can put these boards to work for you in the classroom. It also includes many timesaving tips and a basic list of materials.
- Chapter 2 explains how to prepare the *challenges*, which are the foci of active bulletin boards.
- Chapter 3 presents step-by-step procedures for preparing the bulletin board *assemblies*.
- Chapter 4 suggests ideas for giving *directions*.
- Chapter 5 presents eight types of *answer keys*.
- Chapter 6 gives eight *recordkeeping* methods.
- Chapter 7 puts it all together and shows many *sample bulletin boards* for you to copy or modify.
- Chapter 8 suggests ways to stretch *classroom display space.*
- Chapter 9 contains ideas for *special displays*.
- Chapter 10 gives a number of *storage* suggestions for your reusable bulletin boards.

Our ideas are designed to be extended, transformed, and adapted to your classroom needs. Although our areas of emphasis are math, reading, and language, the active bulletin board techniques of *Teaching Off the Wall* can be applied to any curriculum area and can be used easily as learning centers or activity stations.

Once you have developed your new bulletin board routines you will find they are done easily. Your teaching objectives will suggest themes; our plans will provide the format.

You'll find that the heightened reactions of your students will give you added incentive. Your active bulletin boards will provide a change of pace for all your students and an opportunity for especially active children to leave their seats and participate in pleasurable learning situations. You will have added a valuable element to your teaching repertoire. Creating bulletin boards with important learning devices will give meaning to a task that in the past seemed nothing more than busy work.

Active bulletin boards can turn your classroom walls into important tools for learning. Tantalizing as a puzzle or a game, they command attention and stimulate the student's desire to get involved in the learning task. The active bulletin board *teaches* because it directly involves the student. It presents a cognitive task, which we call a *challenge*. The student is given a way to respond to the challenge by manipulating elements of the *assembly*. Each assembly presents a number of components that can be moved or written upon to indicate the student's answer choices; each board includes the correct *answers for self-checking*. All assemblies provide an intriguing *action* that students find irresistible.

OBJECTIVES Active bulletin boards will meet a number of the *general objectives* that you have for your students. They will:

1. Provide motivation
2. Stimulate curiosity
3. Reinforce (or check) skills
4. Enrich and extend concepts
5. Provide productive outlets for the energetic child

Your specific teaching goals and the particular needs of your students will suggest the themes for these active boards.

How do you know that your objectives are being met? Each active bulletin board has a *self-checking technique* as an integral part of the design. Lifting a flap, turning a dial, or matching a prepared answer key are a few of the checking methods you can choose. *Easy-to-use recordkeeping ideas* complete the plan and allow you to monitor participation.

CLASSROOM MANAGEMENT Now that you have a new kind of interaction in your room, you will want to vary your management techniques to accommodate and encourage it. These active bulletin boards will cause exciting changes in your classroom; traffic patterns, social interaction, and the general mood will be affected by this active participation. Be prepared to help your students to enjoy it.

Here are some tips to make the transition smooth:
1. When you unveil a new bulletin board with a new challenge, give a short pep talk to present the idea.
2. Later, casual references to the new board will alert the group that you expect them to give it a try.
3. Establish behavior guidelines according to the type of challenge you have chosen. Discuss the use and care of the materials you have prepared.
4. Decide if your objective necessitates that all participate. Otherwise use an if-you-have-time approach.
5. A small sign can be used to limit the number of "players" or the time; you may prefer verbal directions.
6. Keep the testing/checking-up informal to encourage the reticent students.

HOW TO USE THIS BOOK
1. Gather together the *materials and supplies* itemized in the next section.
2. Select a *subject area*.
3. Decide on a *specific learning objective*.
4. Choose from the *challenges* a task that will fulfill that objective. (Early selection of the challenge will inspire you and guide you in quick construction of the bulletin board.)
5. Choose an *assembly* that fits the challenge.
6. Use a *theme of interest* to tie everything together.
7. Choose an *answer key*.
8. Choose an appropriate *records plan*.
9. Go to your box of supplies and begin!

SUPPLIES It's a real timesaver to accumulate all your supplies in advance. Use a box or plastic tub that can be stored near the bulletin boards, and try to keep all the supplies for bulletin boards only. Hunting for a necessary item can destroy your own motivation for producing active bulletin boards. An ideal collection of supplies includes the following.

- Rubber cement
- Scissors (embroidery and shears)
- Utility knife (X-ACTO® type)
- Stapler (swing type)
- Pushpins
- Thumbtacks
- Felt-tip markers (washable and permanent)
- Meter or yard stick
- Clear *Con-Tact*® vinyl
- Hole punch

- Crayons
- Cellophane tape
- Brads

Other supplies that are useful, but not necessary, include the following.

- Staple puller
- Stapling gun
- T-square
- Art gum eraser
- Chalk
- Colored pencils
- String
- Precut letters
- Balsa wood
- Yarn

PICTURE AND IDEA FILE   You can save a lot of time by developing a simple filing system for pictures and ideas. All you need are regular- or legal-size manila folders filed alphabetically by topics to suit your needs. When you find an idea that appeals to you, immediately cut it out and set it aside for filing. You will find ideas in magazines, catalogs, sales brochures, comic books, coloring books, and teacher-related materials. Ask your local librarian to save old magazines for you, and don't overlook the magazines that you would not ordinarily read. Avoid the "Where did I see that clever idea?" feeling by keeping your filing system current.

Don't let detail or complexity stop you from choosing an intricate cartoon or drawing. The *overhead transparency method* presented in *Con-Tact®: Classroom Graphics with Con-Tact® Brand Vinyl* (Ruth E. Stiehl, Fearon-Pitman Publishers, Inc., 1978, pp. 6–7) allows you instantly to make anything that catches your eye.

Visit your school's media center and become familiar with its resources. The professionally prepared pictures (SVE, for example) may fit a topic in which you are interested.

MAKING CAPTIONS   The original timesaver for bulletin boards is freehand cutting of captions. You can do it! With your trusty scissors and these steps you can produce high quality lettering quickly without tedious measuring.

1. *Fold your paper* into strips of the letters' height.

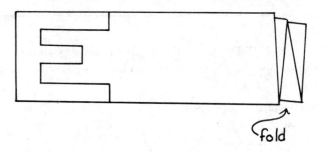

2. *Cut one rectangle* of the desired width through all the thicknesses and use this as a template for cutting the remainder of your basic letter blocks.

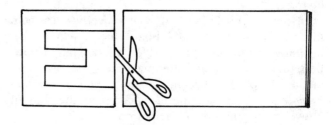

3. *Follow the illustration* to cut the required letters from your basic letter blocks. Cut a T or an I first to determine the thickness of the letter strokes. Soon you will be able to "eyeball" the thickness with ease.

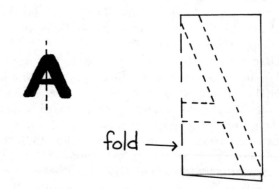

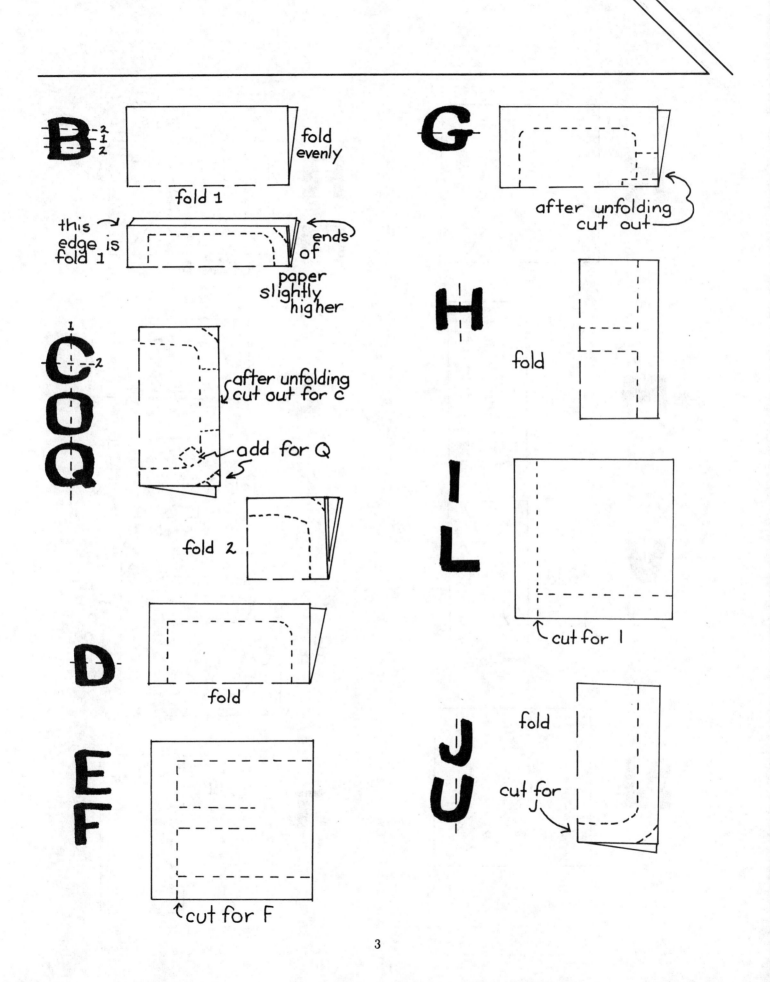

B 2 1 2

fold evenly

fold 1

this edge is fold 1

ends of paper slightly higher

C 1 2

C O Q

after unfolding cut out for c

add for Q

fold 2

D

fold

E

F

cut for F

G

after unfolding cut out

H

fold

I L

cut for 1

J U

fold

cut for J

3

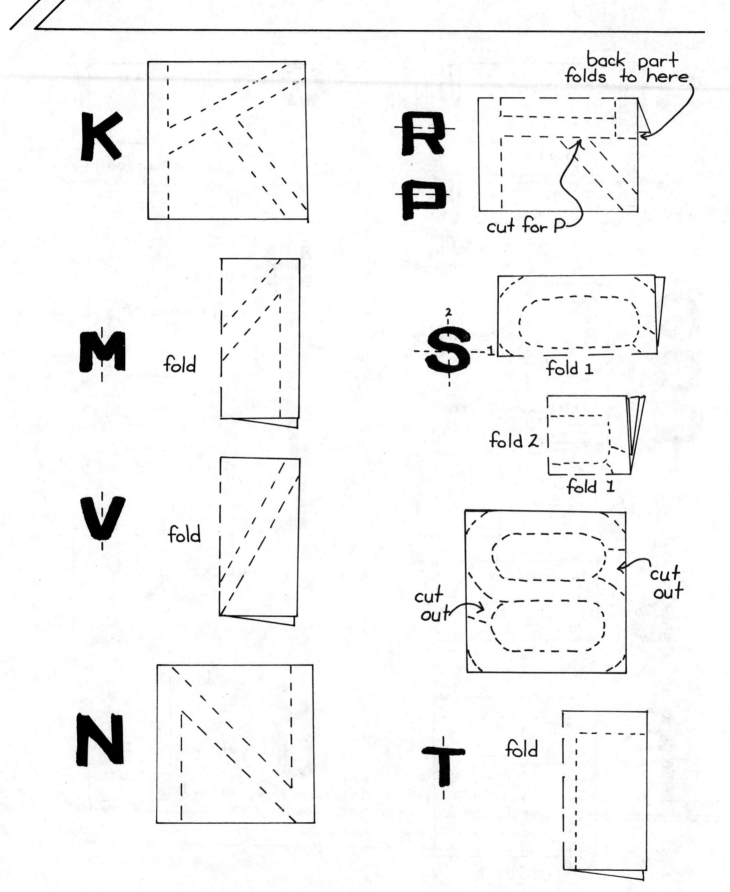

4. Unobtrusively *slit loop letters* like A, B, P, O, and R to cut out the openings.
5. *Begin a backlog* of already prepared blocks in various colors. Store them in envelopes in your supplies box.

ALPHABET VARIATIONS

Rounded lettering

Angular lettering

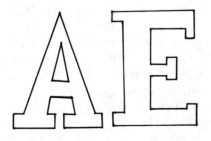

Square lettering

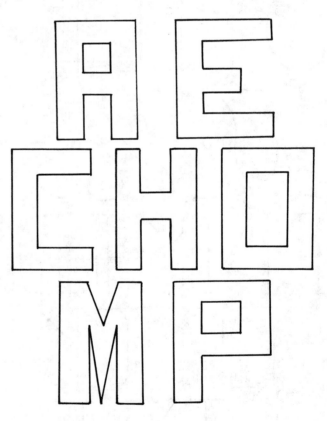

Shadow lettering can be done by using two contrasting colors of paper and cutting two letters at once. Staple these to your board so that the edge of the underneath letter is showing.

Colored tape can be used for quick letters if funds are no problem.

DOUBLE QUICK CAPTIONS Choose an appropriate type of printing—perhaps one of those in the illustration. Lightly write your title in pencil, then trace with a marker. Cut out your caption in a block, free-form, or cartoon-balloon shape.

LETTERING TIPS

1. The type of lettering should be consistent throughout the board. Mix-and-match styles lack unity and may detract from each other.
2. Vertical placement can be difficult to read.
3. Letters are spaced according to their shapes. Round letters are positioned a little closer to each other than straight letters. Irregular letters like J, K, and L can be placed closer together.
4. Space words evenly.
5. Arrange letters and all other components with thumbtacks before you staple.

The challenges are at the heart of this plan for involving students in bulletin-board learning. This chapter describes eight challenges designed to stimulate student participation, interaction, and self-motivation. If you choose one of the challenges to fit a particular teaching objective, you will find that the title, theme, and construction of the bulletin board display will follow readily. Challenges can be easily adapted to any curriculum area.

1 ► MATCH-UP

Matching, or making sets, is a basic skill that can be used in a variety of ways. This is the most versatile of the challenges and the most easily prepared. Choose sets that fit your learning objective: words with words, statements with statements, words with pictures, and other combinations suggested by your objective.

OBJECTIVE To show knowledge of common trees.

PROCEDURE Collect a representative sample of common local tree leaves or make cutouts of them; make cutouts of their names.

CHALLENGE Student matches leaves with names.

BOARDS 1, 2, 3, 4, 5, 6, 7

ASSEMBLIES 1, 2, 3, 4, 5, 6, 12

Note: See *Putting It All Together* (Chapter 1) and *Assemblies* (Chapter 3) for numbered boards and assemblies.

2 ► FILL IN THE BLANKS

This challenge stimulates recall and/or interpretation of facts. It presents possible conclusions and asks the student to select the appropriate answer to fill in the blank.

OBJECTIVE To demonstrate the rules for forming plurals.

PROCEDURE Make a list of nouns meant to be plural and provide the correct choices of endings.

Two monkey____	s
Three country____	ies
Four calf____	ves
Five brush____	es

CHALLENGE Student fills in blank with correct plural form.

ASSEMBLIES 8, 10, 11, 13

BOARDS 8, 9, 10, 11, 12

3 ► YES OR NO

Challenge the student to accept or reject items according to certain evident criteria. The items can be pictures, statements, words, or a combination of these. The student must give a yes or no answer.

OBJECTIVE To review knowledge of derived forms.

PROCEDURE Prepare a list of genuine and invented derived forms; provide yes and no answers.

Arrangement	yes
Skillful	yes
Dreamy	yes
Respectment	no
Resistful	no
Mealy	yes
Inclinement	no

CHALLENGE Student puts a yes by the genuine forms and a no by the invented ones.

ASSEMBLIES 1, 2, 5, 7, 10, 11, 13

BOARDS 13, 14

4 ► SORT OUT

This challenge gives the student practice in categorization. Objects, statements, words, or pictures may be sorted into appropriate categories. *Sort Out* can be structured in any one of three ways.

You supply the categories and the responses; the student places the responses in the correct categories.

OBJECTIVE To show knowledge of the divisibility rules for 2 and 3.

PROCEDURE Prepare a set of numbers that fit each category, using the skill level of your group as your guide.

Divisible by 2	By 3	By 2 and 3*
22	33	24
68	93	54
212	219	216

*A number divisible by 2 and 3 is also divisible by 6.

CHALLENGE Place the numbers in their correct categories. (The physical operation required varies with the kind of assembly used.)

You supply the categories and terms without differentiation. The student must decide which are categories and which are items that belong to each category.

OBJECTIVE To show knowledge of geographical terms.

PROCEDURE Prepare lists of categories and terms and intermingle them. (Here we have indicated the categories by dots.)

Mountains	Bays ·
• Land forms	Rivers
Continents	Estuary
Peninsula	• Bodies of water
Plateau	Delta
Isthmus	Oceans

CHALLENGE Students identify the categories and arrange the terms around them. This could be extended by adding the *Match-Up* challenge, using pictures or drawings that must be matched with the terms.

You supply the categories and items already sorted, but each category has extraneous items that must be removed.

OBJECTIVE To show knowledge of animal classification.

PROCEDURE Prepare and categorize animal groups and names using either words or pictures; insert incorrect items within each category.

Amphibians	Reptiles	Mammals
Frog	Snake	Horse
Salamander	• Whale	Kangaroo
• Chameleon	• Opossum	Bat
Alligator	Box turtle	• Newt
Toad	Lizard	Tiger

CHALLENGE Students remove the incorrectly placed items.

ASSEMBLIES 1, 2, 3, 6, 11

BOARDS 15, 16

8

5 ► ARRANGE PARTS

This challenge suggests a desired outcome, and students must manipulate the parts of the assembly to reach this outcome. It is useful in helping students to synthesize new information.

OBJECTIVE To construct complex sentences.

PROCEDURE Prepare sets of words that can be arranged into complex sentences: her, Sue, umbrella, uses, raining, when, it's. (Sue uses her umbrella when it's raining.)

CHALLENGE Students form a complex sentence.

ASSEMBLIES 1, 2, 3, 6, 11

BOARDS 17, 18

6 ► ORDER IT

This challenge calls upon the student to place items in a predetermined sequence. The sequence may be alphabetical, chronological, rank ordered by importance, mathematical, spatial (a tree from roots to crown or the planets from the sun outward), or mechanical (steps to be followed, as in building a house).

OBJECTIVE To order chronologically the events leading up to the Civil War.

PROCEDURE Prepare a list of events: Missouri Compromise, Garrison founds *Liberator*, Nullification Crisis, Kansas-Nebraska Act, Dred Scott Decision, and John Brown's raid at Harper's Ferry.

CHALLENGE Student arranges the events in chronological order.

ASSEMBLIES 1, 2, 3, 6, 11

BOARDS 19, 20

7 ► WRITE IT

This challenge takes advantage of the student's inclination to write on walls. Using our construction techniques, this board can be erased and recycled for the next student. Sequencing, map reading, and measuring skills are easily adapted to this board concept, or the task may be to create or embellish something, or to play a game.

OBJECTIVE To use metric units in accurate measurements.

PROCEDURE Prepare several items for the student to measure to a specified degree of accuracy.

CHALLENGE Student measures the objects and records answers on the board.

ASSEMBLIES 9, 10, 13, 14, 15, 16

BOARDS 21, 22, 23, 24

8 ► COPY IT

This challenge strengthens the skills of figure-ground perception and spatial orientation. It presents a collection of items for the student to copy or to top with identical shapes.

OBJECTIVE To identify circles, rectangles, and triangles.

PROCEDURE Prepare a drawing as a model for copying and a list of "how many" questions to be answered after the copying is completed. (See example on page 10.)

CHALLENGE Student correctly reproduces the drawing and answers the questions.

ASSEMBLIES 14, 15, 16

BOARDS 25, 26

DRAW THIS FACE

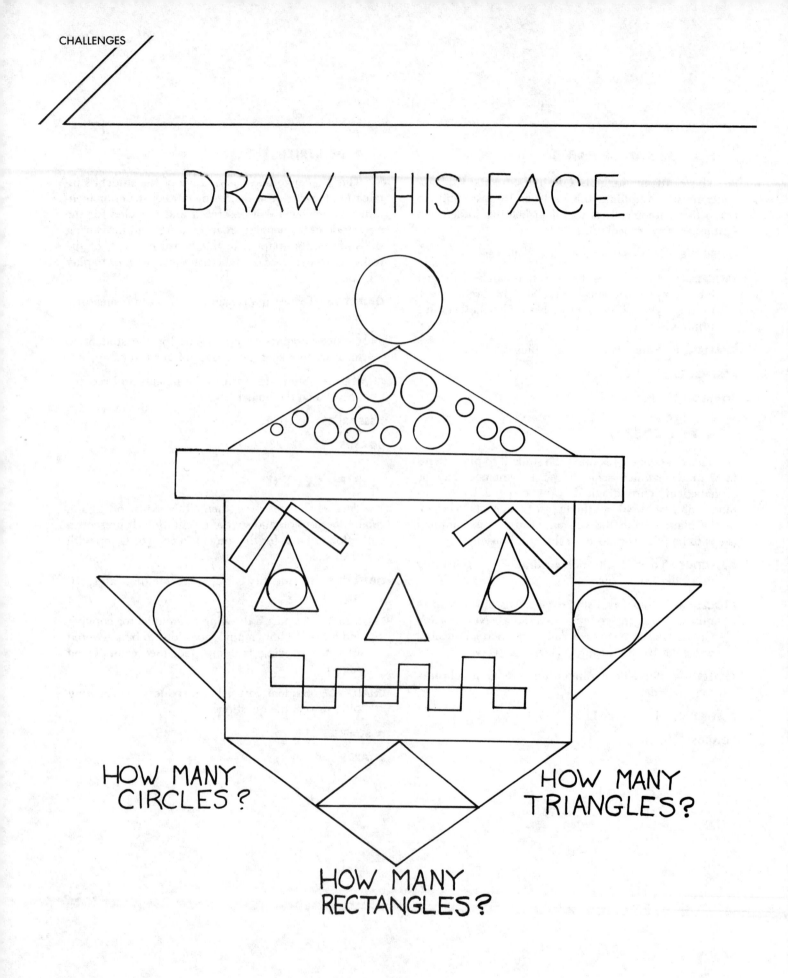

HOW MANY
CIRCLES?

HOW MANY
TRIANGLES?

HOW MANY
RECTANGLES?

Assemblies put your challenge into action. The assembly you choose determines the specific interaction of your students with the bulletin board. Each of the assemblies described here can be used for more than one challenge, and some can be used to record answers as well. With your specific objectives in mind, you can use these assemblies to combine several ideas for a great variety of presentations. A good supply of working parts will attract the students to the board, and many of the items are reusable.

When you are deciding which assembly to use, keep these tips in mind:

1. Most assemblies suggest using written material, but pictures may be more suitable for your objective or for the age level of your students.
2. Measurements are approximate, as bulletin boards vary in size.
3. You can always adapt our constructions to the supplies available to you.

1 ► POCKETS AND SLOTS

This assembly consists of answer cards, slots for answers, and a storage pocket.

SPECIAL MATERIALS Tagboard (stiff paper)

PROCEDURE

1. Cut answer cards from tagboard, using the length of a typical answer for size. Write your answer choices along the long edge, leaving the lower half of the card blank.

2. Cut strips for slots. Strips should be the same length as the answer cards and half as wide, so that answers will be visible when cards are in the slots.

3. Staple the slots to the board where the answers should appear. Be sure to staple along the bottom only, so that cards may be inserted at the top.

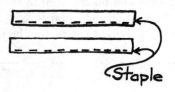

4. Make a pocket from a rectangle of tagboard by folding the piece one-third of the way from the end. The finished size of the pocket should be at least the size of an answer card.

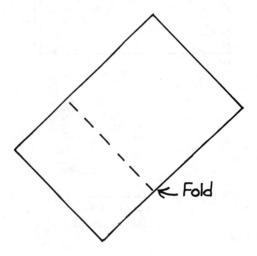

5. Staple the edges of the pocket together, then position the pocket and staple it to the board.

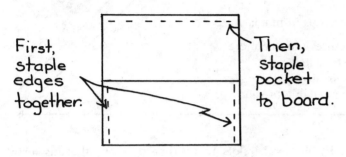

First, staple edges together.

Then, staple pocket to board.

ACTIVITY The student takes the answer cards out of the storage pocket and places them in the correct slots. After the student checks for accuracy, the cards are returned to the pocket, ready for the next student.

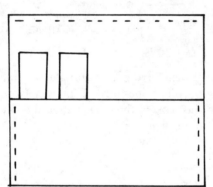

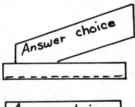

2 ► FELT STICK-ONS

Felt-backed answer cards and a flannel or felt-covered board are the basic components of this assembly.

SPECIAL MATERIALS Tagboard (stiff paper)
Felt and/or flannel (the art department may have scraps)

PROCEDURE

1. Cut out answer cards, using the length of a typical answer as a guide. Write answer choices on them.

2. For each answer card, cut a piece of felt slightly smaller than the card.

3. Glue the felt to the back of the answer card.

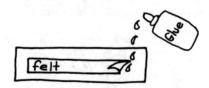

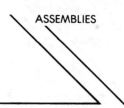

4. Cut a piece of flannel large enough to accommodate all the cards at once; or, cut pieces the size of an answer card. Position and staple these felt pieces to the board where the answers are needed.

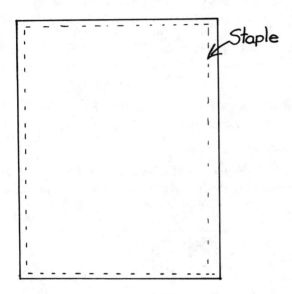

5. Construct a storage pocket like the one in *1 Pockets and Slots* and staple it to the board.

ACTIVITY The student takes the answer cards from the storage pocket and places them in the correct answer position, using a slight downward pressure so the cards will adhere. After the student checks for accuracy, the cards are returned to the pocket, ready for the next student.

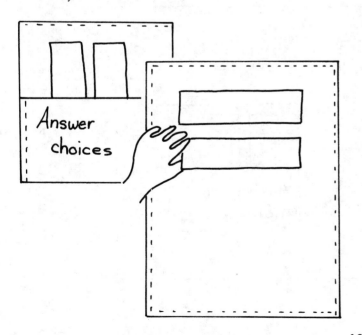

3 ► HOOKS AND PUSHPINS

In this assembly, answer cards are suspended from hooks or pushpins. If you have a pegboard in your room, use hooks. Pushpins easily adapt this assembly for a regular bulletin board.

SPECIAL MATERIALS Tagboard (stiff paper)

PROCEDURE

1. Cut out answer cards, using the length of a typical answer as a guide. Write answers, or glue pictures, on the lower part of cards.

2. Use cellophane tape to reinforce the center top of the back of each answer card.

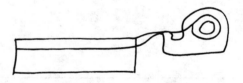

3. Punch a hole larger than the head of the hook in the reinforced area of each answer card.

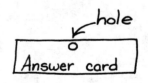

4. Position hooks or pushpins on the pegboard or bulletin board.

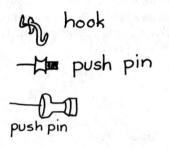

hook

push pin

push pin

5. Construct a storage pocket like the one in *1 Pockets and Slots*. If you are using a pegboard, reinforce the top edge of the pocket and then punch two evenly spaced holes there. Either pin or hook the pocket to the board.

ACTIVITY To display answers, the student suspends the answer cards on the correct hooks. After checking for accuracy, the student returns the cards to the pocket, ready for the next student.

4 ▶ STRINGS ALONE

In this assembly the answer cards are stationary and strings are used to connect or match them. One end of the string may be permanently attached, or all strings may be stored on a hook or pushpin when not in use (depending on whether a pegboard or regular bulletin board is available). The varying lengths of the strings serve as an instant self-check; some students may use them as clues to the correct responses.

SPECIAL MATERIALS   Heavy string or rug yarn
Items to be matched

PROCEDURE

1. Prepare items to be matched and staple or tape them to the bulletin board. Place a hook or a pushpin beside each item.

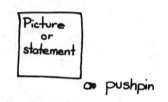

Picture
or
statement

pushpin

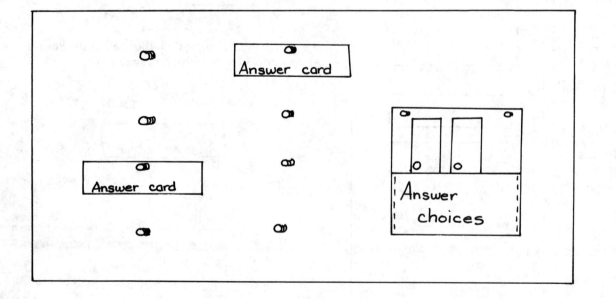

2. Cut lengths of string or yarn to match the distances between the items to be matched, allowing extra for making attachment loops. Make loops at both ends of the string, adjusting lengths so that each string will be taut when fastened to the correct match.

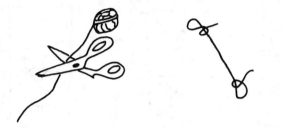

3. Fasten one loop of each string to the appropriate hook or pushpin, letting the other end hang freely; or suspend all strings from the storage hook or pushpin and allow the student to make the entire match.

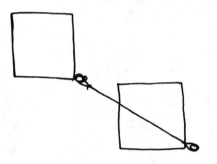

VARIATION For pegboards, you can use pieces of elastic with cafe rings sewn to each end. The lengths will not give clues to the correct matches, and the elastics can be reused.

ACTIVITY The student matches items by attaching the loops. After checking for accuracy, the student returns the strings to their original positions.

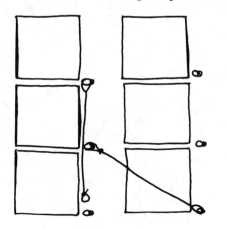

5 ► SLIDING ARROWS

In this assembly, students move arrows along paper or string guides to indicate the correct responses.

SPECIAL MATERIALS Tagboard (stiff paper)

PROCEDURE

1. Cut arrows or triangles from tagboard to serve as markers.

2. Cut guide strips from tagboard. Make them about 5 cm (2 in.) longer than the entire list of choices. The width of the guide strip should be half the length of the arrow shaft.

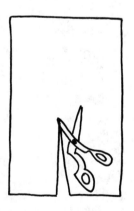

3. Reinforce the back of each arrow with cellophane tape. Make two slits in each arrow as shown. They should be 2½ cm (1 in.) apart, and long enough to slide over guide strips.

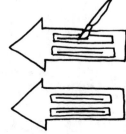
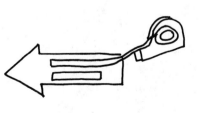

4. Thread each strip through the slits in an arrow. Lengthen the slit if the arrow does not move easily. Staple the ends of the strips to the board next to the appropriate choices.

ACTIVITY The student moves the arrows to indicate responses. The arrows are returned to a rest position after answers are checked.

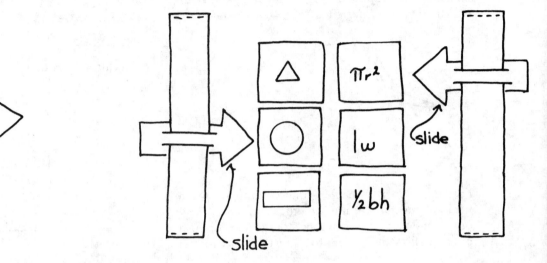

VARIATION Use lengths of string for the guides, and reinforce and punch holes in the arrows. If necessary, tie knots in the string at each choice position.

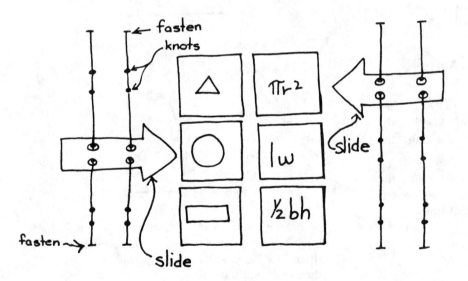

6 ► PINCH-ON CLOTHESPINS

Answers on clothespins are clipped to the correct places in this assembly, which is best suited to short answers.

SPECIAL MATERIALS   Tagboard (stiff paper)
  Pinch-type clothespins

PROCEDURE

1. Cut answer cards no larger than the clothespins.

2. Write answers on the cards and tape each card to a clothespin.

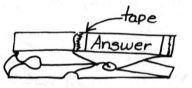

3. Make holding strips from tagboard for the clothespins. Staple holding strips beside each set of cards to match, keeping staples along one edge to create a flap for clipping.

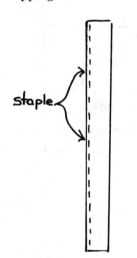

4. Use one long holding strip for storing clothespins when not in use, or construct a storage pocket like the one in *1 Pockets and Slots*.

VARIATION   For a challenge that involves sentence construction or longer answers, use long pieces of tagboard for holding strips.

ACTIVITY   The student clips the clothespins to the holding strips to show correct responses. Clothespins are returned to the storage strip or pocket after checking.

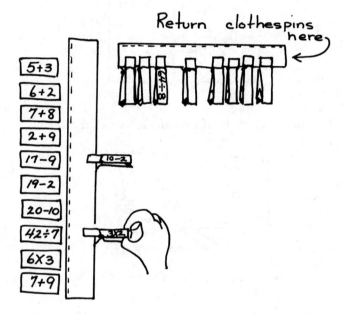

7 ► COVER-UPS

In this assembly, answer choices are indicated by covering up the incorrect responses with cards.

SPECIAL MATERIALS Tagboard (stiff paper)

PROCEDURE

1. Prepare answer choices and place them on the bulletin board.

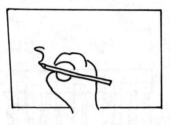

2. Cut out cards to fit over the incorrect choices.

3. Cut narrow strips of tagboard to hold the cover-up cards. You can use a paper cutter as a timesaver.

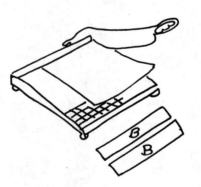

4. Staple holding strips on either side of each answer choice. Be sure to staple along outer and lower edges only.

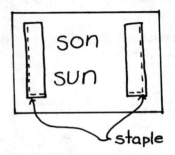

5. Construct a storage pocket like the one in *1 Pockets and Slots.*

ACTIVITY The student displays the correct choices by slipping the cover-up cards over the incorrect ones. After checking for accuracy, the student returns the cover-up cards to the storage pocket.

8 ► TURNING DIALS

In this assembly, two concentric circles are fastened to the board by placing a brad through their centers. The answers are printed on the bottom circle, and a window cut in the top circle can be dialed to reveal the answers.

SPECIAL MATERIALS   Tagboard (stiff paper)
Compass or circle patterns

PROCEDURE

1. Cut two circles from tagboard, one of which is about 5 cm (2 in.) smaller in diameter, and mark the centers. (The top and bottom of a round wastebasket make quick patterns.)

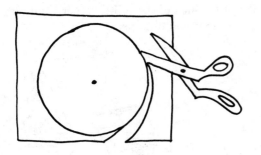

2. To make an answer window, cut a wedge-shaped opening in the smaller circle about 2½ cm (1 in.) from the edge. The size of the opening is determined by the length of your answers. Do not cut into the center.

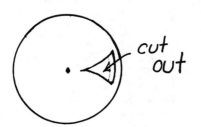

3. Using the answer window as your guide, write answer choices on the larger circle. Use a brad to fasten the two circles together at the center.

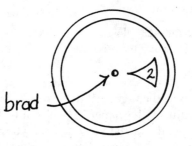

4. Position circles and fasten them to the board, stapling around the edge of the larger circle.

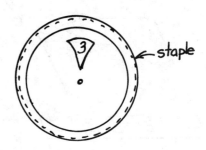

VARIATION   Dials may be used as spinners for board games. Simply write numbers around the circumference of the larger circle. The players close their eyes and turn the smaller circle to find the number of spaces to move. Dials can be reused, especially if they are covered with clear vinyl.

ACTIVITY   The student turns the inner circle to reveal the correct choice. After checking for accuracy, the student may move the dial to a random position.

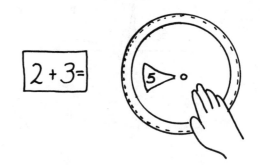

9 ► WATCH IT GROW

Using a continuous roll of paper, this assembly allows the student to make measurements or display certain information.

SPECIAL MATERIALS   Tagboard (large piece)
Paper for rolls (two colors)

PROCEDURE

1. Cut slits in the tagboard that are a little longer than the width of the paper. The distance between the slits depends on the viewing area you need for the material on the paper. Reinforce the slits with tape, or cover the entire tagboard with clear vinyl.

2. From each color, cut a piece of roll paper that is 2¹/₂ cm (1 in.) longer than the distance between the slits in the tagboard. Write a measurement scale, or other information, on one piece only.

3. Securely tape the two colors of roll paper together at one end only. Cover the entire surface with clear vinyl for strength and flexibility.

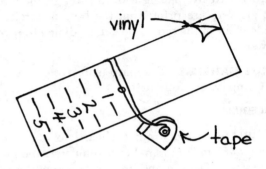

4. Thread the roll paper through the slits, then tape the other ends of the roll together. You now have a continuous roll of paper.

5. Staple the assembly to the board as shown.

VARIATIONS   Leave the two-color roll blank and put the measurements on the tagboard. The day's temperature or the weekly average test score can be displayed. Group a number of rolls and create bar graphs for various kinds of information.

ACTIVITY   Using the bottom slit as a baseline, students align items with the roll. Then they press the roll upward until the measurement column is precisely aligned with the top of the item being measured. The correct measurement can then be read at the baseline.

10 ► FOLD-UPS

In this assembly, flaps are used to cover incorrect responses.

SPECIAL MATERIALS   Tagboard (stiff paper)

PROCEDURE

1. Cut cards as illustrated, and write correct and incorrect responses on them as shown.

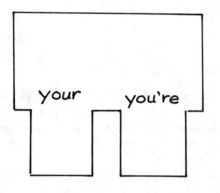

2. Score the fold lines and reinforce with tape. Cut slits to hold the corners of the flaps when they are in the cover-up position.

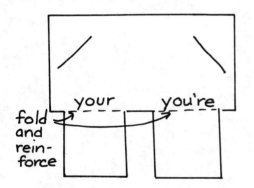

3. Staple cards to boards in desired positions.

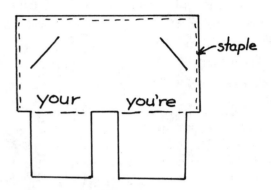

ACTIVITY   As students make a choice, they fold flaps up to cover incorrect responses. After checking for accuracy, the student returns the flaps to the down position.

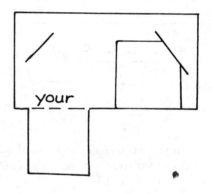

21

11 ► MAGIC MAGNETS

In this assembly, magnets adhere to staples and mark correct answers.

SPECIAL MATERIALS Construction paper
Magnets (small kitchen type)

PROCEDURE

1. Write your challenges and answer choices on construction-paper cards.

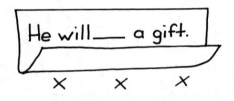

2. Position and mark the locations of the answer choices on the bulletin board.

3. Make a clump of staples in the areas of the correct answer (for instant checking) or under each answer (if using an answer key).

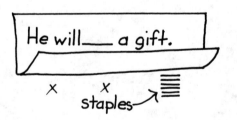

4. Reposition the cards so that the answer choices are over the clumps of staples and fasten to the board.

5. Prepare a storage pocket to hold the magnets (see *1 Pockets and Slots*) or make a storage area from a large clump of staples.

ACTIVITY The student uses the magnets to indicate correct choices. After checking for accuracy, the student returns magnets to the storage pocket or storage area.

12 ► CIRCLING ARROWS

In this assembly, arrows radiating from a central point mark answers, indicate matches, or show choices.

SPECIAL MATERIALS Tagboard (stiff paper)
Brads, 5 cm (2 in.) or longer

PROCEDURE

1. Cut an arrow for each response, using the size of your responses as a guide. Save scraps.

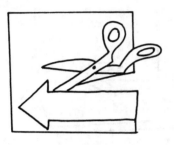

2. Reinforce the back end of each arrow shaft with cellophane tape.

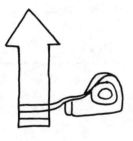

3. Punch a hole through the shaft of each arrow. Write responses on arrows as shown.

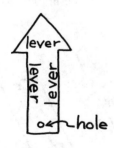

4. Cut a square of tagboard that is smaller than the length of an arrow and punch a hole in its center. Fasten the arrows to the tagboard square with a brad.

5. Staple the square to the board. Prepare and position the matches for the arrows; staple them to the board. Cut rectangles from the scraps of tagboard to make stops for the arrows and staple a stop next to each match.

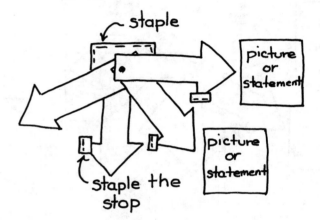

ACTIVITY Students move the arrows to show responses, using the stops to keep the arrows in place. Arrows are returned to a random pattern after checking accuracy.

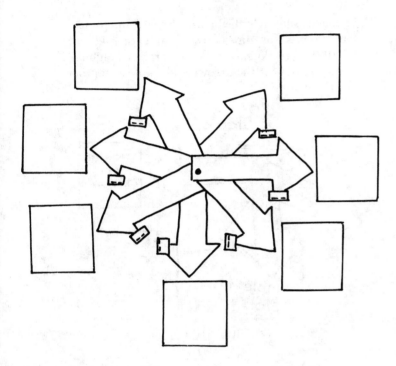

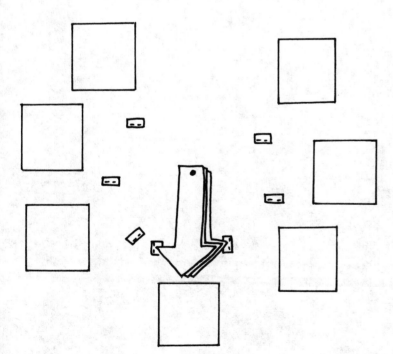

13 ► SLIDING PARTS

In this assembly, sliding strips are manipulated to reveal information. The strips narrow the students' field of vision, allowing them to concentrate on specific items.

SPECIAL MATERIALS Tagboard (stiff paper)

PROCEDURE

1. Cut strips to carry information.

2. Cut strip holders. Then cut horizontal slits in them to accommodate the strips.

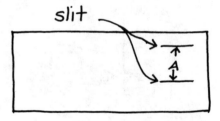

3. Write information on the strips, using the distance between the slits in the holders as a frame.

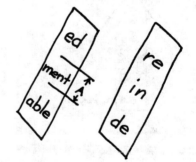

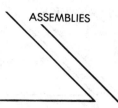

4. Insert the strips through the slits in the strip holders and staple holders to the board as shown.

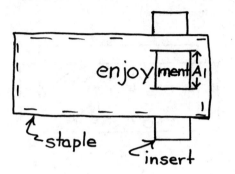

ACTIVITY The student slides the strips through the holders to reveal information frame by frame and make selections. After checking for accuracy, the student returns the strips to starting positions for the next student. (*Note:* Challenge the students to supply and record the information necessary for the sliding parts.)

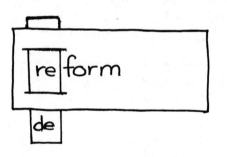

14 ► TEAR-OFFS

Worksheets are stapled to the board. Instructions may be individualized or general and may be written on each sheet or on another part of the board.

SPECIAL MATERIALS Sheets of paper

PROCEDURE

1. Record the instructions on each sheet—one per student—or number each sheet if giving individualized instructions.

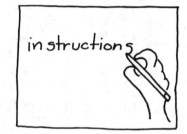

2. Staple the last page to the board first, at the top edge only. (You are making a pad.) Stagger the placement of the staples to facilitate tearing off as you continue to add pages.

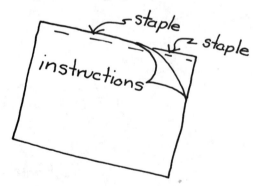

ACTIVITY After following the instructions, students tear off their own sheets so that the board is ready for the next person.

15 ► WIPE-OFFS

Transparent *Con-Tact®* vinyl covers the materials. Marks of grease pencils, crayons, or washable markers can then be wiped away.

SPECIAL MATERIALS Tagboard (stiff paper)
Tissue (dry and wet)

PROCEDURE

1. Prepare the challenge and write it on tagboard.

```
W R O D E E L O S
R I G H T L O N E
I B Y S O N A I P
T Y O C S E N T R
E O W E L O D I O
R C E N T B U Y A
I W S T I D L E D
```

2. Place the tagboard face down on the backing side of the vinyl. Cut the vinyl a little larger than the prepared materials to allow for overlap on the back.

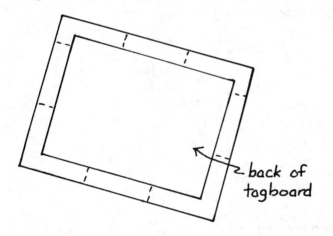

back of tagboard

3. Cut a square from each corner of the vinyl.

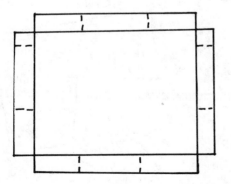

4. Make sure the material is centered on the back of the vinyl, and begin peeling off the backing sheet. Peel and press as you remove the backing sheet to eliminate air bubbles.

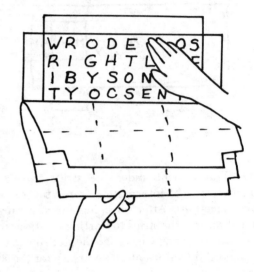

5. Fold the flaps of vinyl to the back and press in place.

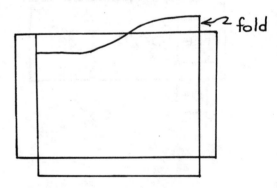

fold

6. Staple the vinyl-covered tagboard to bulletin board.

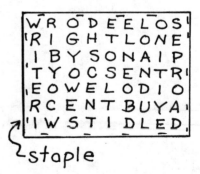

staple

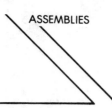

7. Prepare two pockets like the one in *1 Pockets and Slots.* Store student writing materials in one, cleaning materials in the other.

ACTIVITY   Students record their answers on the vinyl with a crayon or washable marker. After checking for accuracy, the student wipes the vinyl clean, ready for the next student. For wiping off the crayon, use a dry tissue. For marker, use a damp tissue.

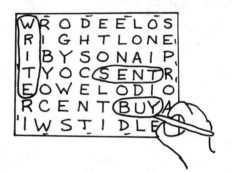

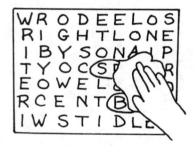

DIRECTIONS:

FIND AND CIRCLE THE WORDS THAT WILL CORRECTLY COMPLETE EACH SENTENCE.

1. Use a pencil to ___.
2. The letter was ___ by air mail.
3. Nancy will ___ a new dress at the store.

16 ► TOUCH AND TELL

A raised shape representing a figure, word, or numeral is hidden by fabric.

SPECIAL MATERIALS   Tagboard (stiff paper)
Cardboard (very thick)
Thin fabric to cover cards
Yarn or heavy string (optional)

PROCEDURE

1. Cut cards to accommodate your hidden material. Choose one of the next two methods for preparing the hidden answers.

2. Outline the letters or shapes on the cards with glue, and lay yarn along the glue lines.

Or cut the letters and shapes out of very thick cardboard and glue to card. (This is recommended for durability.)

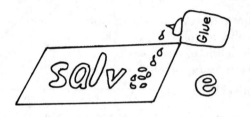

3. Cut fabric a little larger than the cards to allow for folding the edges to the back of the card. Staple the fabric around the edges of the cards, keeping it as taut as possible.

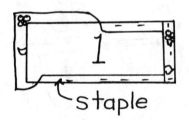

4. Label the top and number each card. Keep a record of what each card contains.

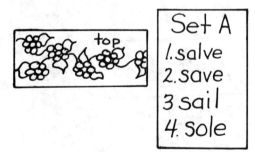

5. Make a storage pocket like the one in *1 Pockets and Slots*, or staple the cards to the board.

ACTIVITY Students identify the hidden material through their sense of touch. They may be looking for a correct match, or simply identifying what you have hidden.

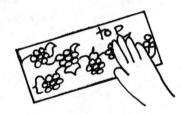

An instructional bonus of active bulletin boards is that they provide painless practice in following directions. *Written directions* have the advantage of being there whenever they are needed by the student. The advantage of *oral directions* is that no advance preparation is necessary.

The complexity of some assemblies necessitates written directions. Your active bulletin board design will usually have one or more written clues. Sometimes these clues will be in the form of a *specific list of steps*. Your students' first experiences with active bulletin boards will be greatly enhanced if you carefully list the steps they should follow. Written directions are needed for these sample boards: *Guinness Goes Metric*, *I Scream You Scream*, and *Mountain Climbing*.

Students may also be clued in to the learning task presented by the board through the use of *captions*. You can use captions to eliminate the need for a separate list of directions. When the action is obvious, all students will need to see is a title. Caption directions are adequate for *Correct the Computer* and *Fill the Hoppers*.

Oral directions, while requiring the least preparation, may be the least effective. Confine oral directions to boards with obvious actions, or use them to supplement written directions.

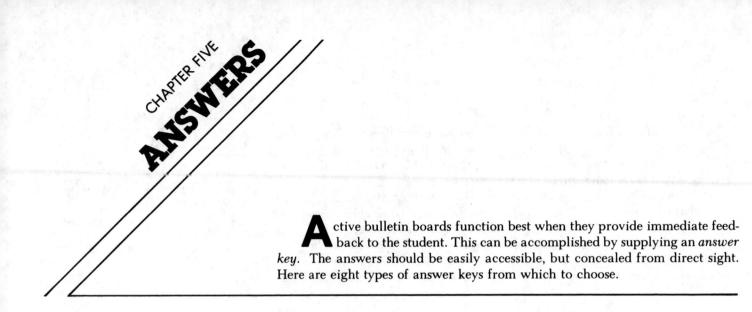

CHAPTER FIVE
ANSWERS

Active bulletin boards function best when they provide immediate feedback to the student. This can be accomplished by supplying an *answer key*. The answers should be easily accessible, but concealed from direct sight. Here are eight types of answer keys from which to choose.

1 ► FLAPS

The basic answer key is a covered list. The student lifts a flap to expose the list of answers. With this method, all answers are located in one place on the board. The key is numbered or otherwise identified to correspond to the challenge.

SPECIAL MATERIALS   Two sheets of paper

PROCEDURE

1. Write the answers on one sheet and number them to correspond to the challenge.

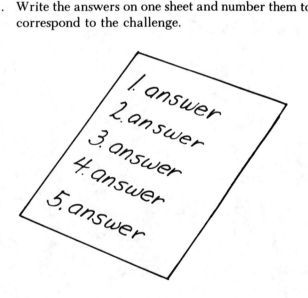

2. Write "Answer Key" on the second sheet to make a cover.

3. Place the cover sheet over the answer sheet, creating a flap, and staple to the board.

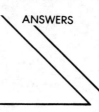

VARIATION Instead of a rectangular shape, use shapes that fit your theme.

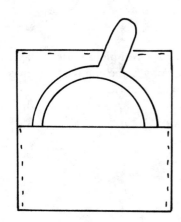

2 ▶ MIRROR IMAGE

This is our students' favorite answer key. Answers are deciphered using a mirror. Answers may be grouped in a central location on the board, or placed next to each part of the challenge.

SPECIAL MATERIALS Sheet of paper
Mirror

PROCEDURE

1. Write answers on the paper, beginning at the right and reversing the letters that are not symmetrical to produce a mirror image. Staple the answers to the board.

2. Place the mirror in a storage pocket like the one in assembly *1 Pockets and Slots.*

31

3. Focus the mirror on the answers to check.

VARIATION Try a complete bulletin board using this method to convey the challenge. It may rank as the best board of the year!

3 ▶ UPSIDE DOWN

In this method, often used in magazines, the answers are placed upside down. The student can turn them right side up by rotating the answer key on a brad.

SPECIAL MATERIALS Tagboard (two sheets)

PROCEDURE

1. Reinforce and punch matching holes in the bottoms of both sheets of tagboard.

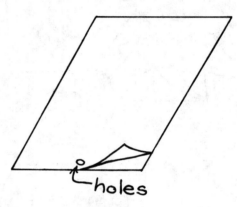

2. With the hole at the bottom, write your answers on one piece of the tagboard.

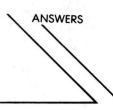

3. Place the answer sheet face up on the backing sheet, align the holes, and fasten with the brad.

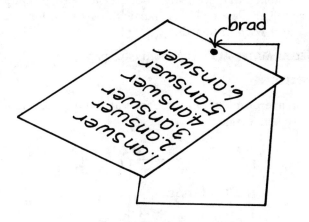

4. Staple the backing sheet to the board so that the answers are upside down and can be rotated on the brad for checking.

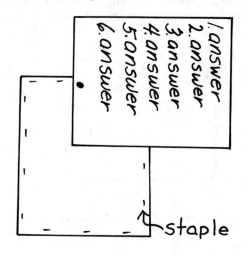

4 ▶ PULL TABS

Here answers are covered with a tab or movable strip and placed next to each challenge or section. The student checks each response immediately by pulling the tab down to expose the correct choice.

SPECIAL MATERIALS   Tagboard (stiff paper)

PROCEDURE

1. Cut a rectangular piece of tagboard for each answer location.

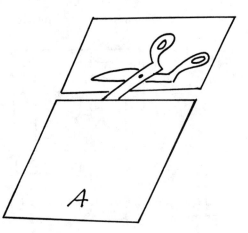

2. Write answers on the cards, centering the material so the tabs will cover it fully.

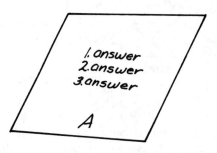

3. Make two slits, wider than the written area, in the bottom of each card.

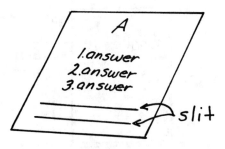

33

4. Cut a tab for each answer card, for most of its length slightly narrower than the slits, and high enough to completely cover the answer area.

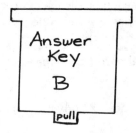

5. Thread the tab through the slits, covering, and answer(s).

6. Staple the answer sheet to the board so that the tab remains movable.

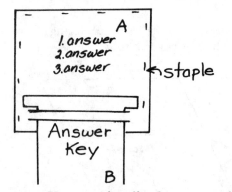

VARIATION Horizontal pull tabs are simpler to construct. Make the tab longer than the width of the paper on which the challenge is written. When stapling the challenge to the board, leave a space between the staples large enough to slip in the tab.

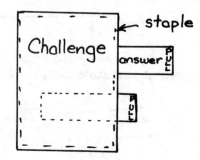

5 ► STENCIL

A stencil that conceals all but the answers is placed over the challenge. This is particularly useful for *Puzzles* and *Write-It* boards.

SPECIAL MATERIALS Tagboard (stiff paper)

PROCEDURE

1. Place pushpins on the board at the top corners of the challenge.

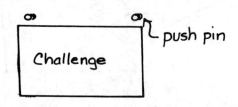

2. Cut a piece of tagboard large enough to fit over the challenge. This will become the stencil. Punch holes in the top corners of the stencil tagboard to hang it on the pushpins.

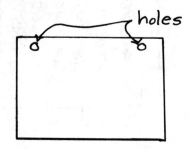

3. Hang the stencil tagboard and lightly trace the places where the correct answers will be.

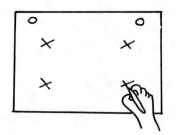

34

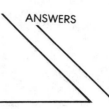

4. On a flat surface, cut out the areas of the correct answer locations.

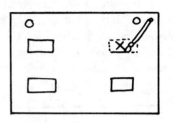

5. Rehang the stencil and check the alignment, adjusting the pushpins as needed.

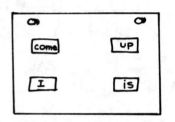

6. Place a pushpin in another area of the board to store the stencil.

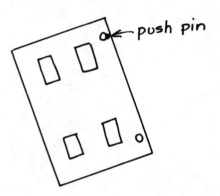

6 ▶ OVERLAYS

A clear plastic overlay allows quick checking. *Copy-It* and *Write-It* challenges are suited to this method.

SPECIAL MATERIALS Clear acetate sheet (overhead projector supplies, or available at office supply or dime stores).

PROCEDURE

1. Place pushpins in the top corners of the work to be checked. Align the acetate over the material and mark pushpin locations.

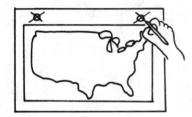

2. Punch holes in the acetate for hanging.

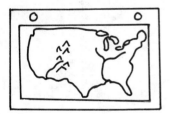

3. Hang the acetate, and record the answer information on it with permanent markers.

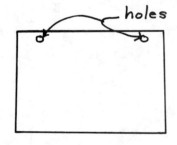

4. Place a pushpin in another area of the board to store the overlay answer key.

7 ► TURNING DIALS

Assembly 8 *Turning Dials* can be adapted as an answer key. In each wedge opening, write an answer. The student turns the dial and the answer appears.

see
1.

8 ► COLORED DOTS

Colored dots are an easily prepared method for checking challenges that involve matching or cards. Identically colored dots (or shapes, or letters) are placed on the corresponding pieces. Develop your own coding system. No special materials are needed.

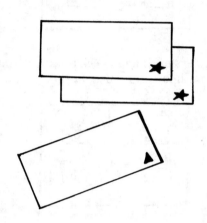

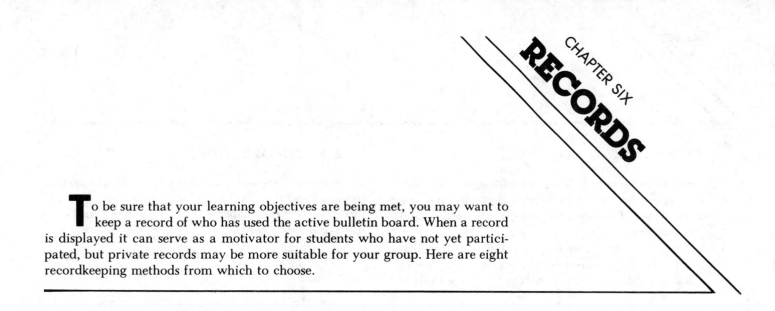

To be sure that your learning objectives are being met, you may want to keep a record of who has used the active bulletin board. When a record is displayed it can serve as a motivator for students who have not yet participated, but private records may be more suitable for your group. Here are eight recordkeeping methods from which to choose.

1 ► AUTOGRAPH SHEET

A sheet of paper is placed on or near the active bulletin board. Colored pencils are provided for the students to sign their names after completing the challenge. (A place to record their scores could be included where it is applicable.)

SPECIAL MATERIALS Construction paper (large sheet)
Colored pencils

PROCEDURE

1. Write the name of the record on the sheet.

2. Staple the sheet to the board, or hang it nearby.

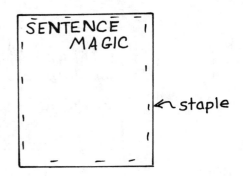

3. Supply colored pencils in a storage pocket like the one in assembly *1 Pockets and Slots.*

4. Students record their names when the work is completed.

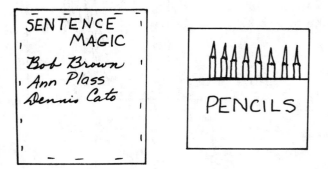

VARIATION

1. Prepare two or more record sheets, labeling each one to represent a level of achievement. Labels could be: Superstars, Experts, and Amateurs; Home run, Triple, Double, and Single; or Champions and Runners-up.
2. Prepare autograph sheets to represent achievement levels using cartoon cutouts instead of titles. Choose cartoon characters with positive character traits.

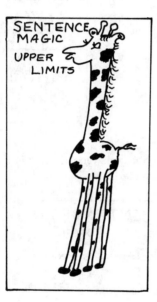

2 ► COLOR BLOCKS

Students color in blocks to show the bulletin boards they have completed. The color block sheet can be re-used if it is covered with clear vinyl and the record kept in washable marker.

SPECIAL MATERIALS   Tagboard (stiff paper)

PROCEDURE

1. Rule the tagboard horizontally and vertically to form blocks. List the student names in the lefthand column. Across the top, list the boards (or numbers to correspond to the boards).
2. Cover the written material with clear vinyl and staple it to the board, or display it nearby.
3. Supply crayons or washable markers in a storage pocket like the one in assembly *1 Pockets and Slots.*

	BOARD NAME	BOARD NAME	BOARD NAME
Bob C.			
Steve R.			
Betty A.			
Meg S.			
Sue			
Ann			
Mike			
Julie			
Mitch			

↖ staple

MARKERS

3 ► SCORE CARDS

Score cards are used when several active bulletin boards are set up simultaneously. Score cards may be displayed in the classroom, or students may have individual ones for private recordkeeping.

SPECIAL MATERIALS   Tagboard (stiff paper)

PROCEDURE
1. Make a tagboard score card for each board with score classifications on each.
2. Cover the score cards with vinyl if you wish.
3. Display cards and provide markers for students' use.

BOARD TITLE			
10 CORRECT	9 CORRECT	8 CORRECT	7 CORRECT
Ann Betty Mike Don	Greg	Bill Neil	Joe Joyce

VARIATION   For individual score cards, make a ditto of the classifications for each student. These may be kept in students' notebooks and checked periodically by the teacher.

MARKERS

4 ► PATH TO A PRIZE

With this excellent motivator, every student must work at the bulletin board to earn a prize for the group. The path is displayed on or near the active bulletin board. As students complete the challenge, they sign their names in crayon in a block. When all have signed and all blocks are filled, the prize has been earned.

SPECIAL MATERIALS Tagboard (stiff paper)

PROCEDURE

1. Draw a path on tagboard, making one square for each student and including a start and finish. (Imitate a board game.) Show what the prize will be.
2. Cover the tagboard with vinyl for reuse.
3. Display the path on a wall or staple it to the board.
4. Construct a storage pocket like the one in assembly *1 Pockets and Slots* to hold crayons or markers.

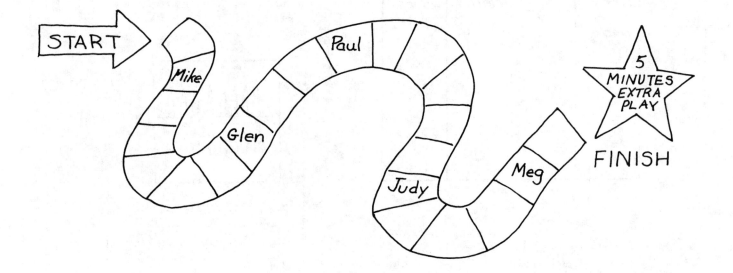

5 ► BUTTONS

A tangible reward sparks interest. Here students complete the challenge, receive a button, and record their names on the button board, which is displayed on or near the active bulletin board. A simple paper button can create a feeling of self-worth!

SPECIAL MATERIALS Tagboard (stiff paper)
Construction paper
Button pattern, 7 cm (3 in.) diameter
Masking tape

PROCEDURE

1. Using the button pattern and construction paper, trace and cut out a button for each student. Write the name of the bulletin board or an appropriate word of achievement on each button.

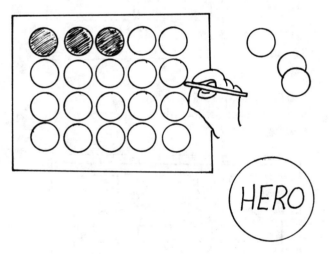

2. Make a button board to display buttons and record names of participants. Using the button pattern, trace a circle for each student on a piece of tagboard. If you wish, cover the button board with clear vinyl.

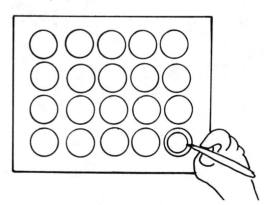

3. From masking tape, make a loop for each button, sticky side out.

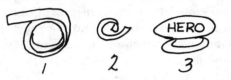

4. Stick a button on each circle of the button board.

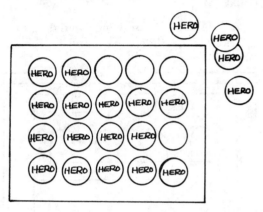

5. Display the button board on a wall or staple it to the bulletin board.

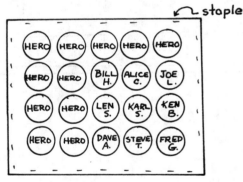

6. When students complete the challenge, they may take a button from the button board and write their name on the exposed circle.

VARIATION For the buttons, use a shape to match the theme of the bulletin board, such as a football, or a pumpkin, or a flower.

6 ► BUILDING BLOCKS

This is an individualized recordkeeping strategy. As students complete work on the board, they color a block on a teacher-prepared ditto. The blocks correspond to individual bulletin boards and are arranged to form a building.

SPECIAL MATERIALS Ditto master
Pen, for drawing on master

PROCEDURE

1. Prepare the ditto by drawing a building of blocks. Directions to the student may be written on the ditto.

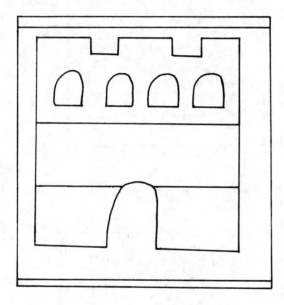

2. Label each block with a bulletin board title, or fill in the titles as the boards are presented, or number each block.

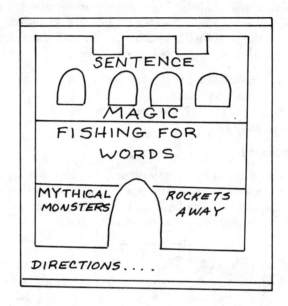

3. Distribute dittos to the students with instructions to color the appropriate block after completing the challenge.

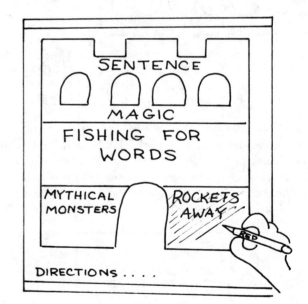

7 ► MYSTERY PICTURE

This is another individualized recordkeeper. When students finish the bulletin board, they color a space or spaces on their own record, which is a mystery picture. When all the board challenges are completed, all the spaces will be colored, revealing the picture.

SPECIAL MATERIALS Ditto master
Pen, for drawing on master
Coloring book, or other picture source

PROCEDURE

1. Prepare a ditto by drawing a picture that has many parts.
2. Assign a number to each color needed to complete the picture, and number the parts by color.
3. Assign a color number to each bulletin board.

4. Distribute the dittos to students, instructing them to color the appropriate spaces as they complete the challenges of each numbered bulletin board. Collect the mystery pictures from time to time to note progress.

NUMBER	COLOR	BOARD TITLE
1	RED	NUMBERS AWAY
2	BLUE	GROW THROUGH READING
3	GREEN	DICTIONARY DASH
4	PURPLE	HOW MANY ?
5	YELLOW	CHAIN OF LIFE
6	BROWN	BARREL OF MONKEYS

8 ► DOT-TO-DOT

This system motivates students to try the challenge because it makes each person responsible for completing a part of a dot-to-dot picture. Reluctant participants want to do their share to complete the picture.

SPECIAL MATERIALS Dot-to-dot puzzle

PROCEDURE

1. Cover a commercially prepared dot-to-dot picture with clear vinyl to allow reuse.
2. List students' names and assign each student two consecutive numbers.
3. Instruct the students to connect their numbers after completing the challenge.

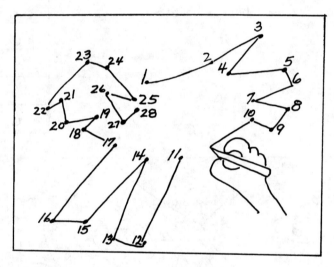

STUDENT NAME	DOTS TO CONNECT
BILL COTTER	1 TO 2
KAREN GLASS	2 TO 3
SUE CATO	3 TO 4
GEORGE SMITH	4 TO 5
ALICE GREEN	5 TO 6
DAVE OWENS	6 TO 7
SOPHIA CROSS	7 TO 8
KEN WEEMS	8 TO 9
LAURIE AMES	9 TO 10
ARTHUR MINK	10 TO 11
JOE MILLER	11 TO 12
MIKE BURROWS	12 TO 13

CHAPTER SEVEN
PUTTING IT TOGETHER

Here is a simple plan for constructing an active bulletin board that includes all the elements we have discussed. With these steps you can quickly and easily produce a board that is suited to your current instructional needs. The best approach is to focus on the learning objective to be implemented by the challenge and on the assemblies that will initiate student response. All other considerations—such as theme, layout, background, and color—will follow naturally.

STEPS TO SUCCESS

1. *Select a subject area* you wish to present.
2. *Choose a learning objective* from the material you are currently teaching. (Do you wish to reinforce a skill, or present a new idea?)
3. *Pick a challenge* from Chapter 2 that is suited to your objective.
4. *Select an assembly* from Chapter 3 that is appropriate to the challenge task.
5. *Choose a theme* that ties the three elements together. A theme can be anything that appeals to your students: sports, entertainment, nature, cartoon characters, current events, and so on. Use your *ideas file* to stimulate your own creativity.
6. *Pick an answer key* from Chapter 5.
7. *Select a records plan* from Chapter 6.
8. *Go to your supplies box* and begin!

PROCEDURE Now, using the tools and materials from your supplies box, make the following.

1. Cards indicating the sentence patterns: N–V, N–V–N, N–LV–N, and N–LV–ADJ.

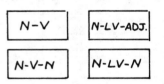

2. Cards on which you print the words to be arranged.

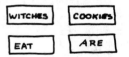

3. Slots to hold the word cards as the sentences are constructed.

4. Pockets to store the word cards.

5. A printed set of instructions on a tagboard ghost.

DIRECTIONS
1. TAKE WORD CARDS AND ARRANGE THEM TO MAKE THE SENTENCES INDICATED.
2. PULL TABS TO CHECK YOUR SENTENCES.
3. WHEN YOU'VE FINISHED ALL THE SENTENCES, TAKE A JACK-O'-LANTERN BUTTON AND WRITE YOUR NAME IN ITS PLACE.

6. A caption and "decorator" items to carry out the theme (such as a haunted house, a witch on a broom, a cooking pot with smoke).

SENTENCE RECIPES

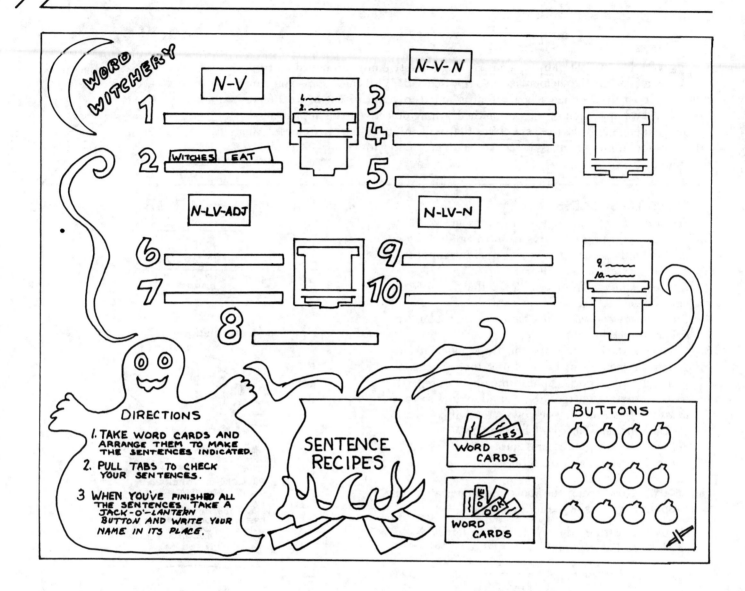

SAMPLE BOARD

SUBJECT Language arts.

OBJECTIVE To review and reinforce understanding of sentence patterns and parts of speech.

CHALLENGE Choose *5 Arrange Parts* to arrive at specified outcomes, sentence patterns. The patterns are noun-verb-noun (N-V-N), noun-verb (N-V), noun–linking verb–noun (N-LV-N), and noun–linking verb–adjective (N-LV-ADJ). Words supplied are to be arranged in these sentence patterns.

ASSEMBLY Select *1 Pockets and Slots.*

THEME The autumn season suggests a Halloween theme, and so you prepare a Halloween word list. (Adding words from current reading selections would enhance your challenge.)

ANSWERS Pick *4 Pull Tabs.*

RECORDS Select *5 Buttons.*

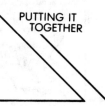

7. Pull tab answer keys.

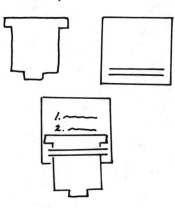

8. Buttons and button board for recordkeeping.

Arrange these items and staple them to the bulletin board, then introduce the board to your class.

THE BULLETIN BOARDS Here are twenty-six sample bulletin boards that combine elements in a variety of ways suited to the desired learning objectives. By the time you have adapted these sample boards to your own needs you will find the procedures have become second nature. Remember that each bulletin board is adaptable to any subject area; subject areas are listed for quick reference only.

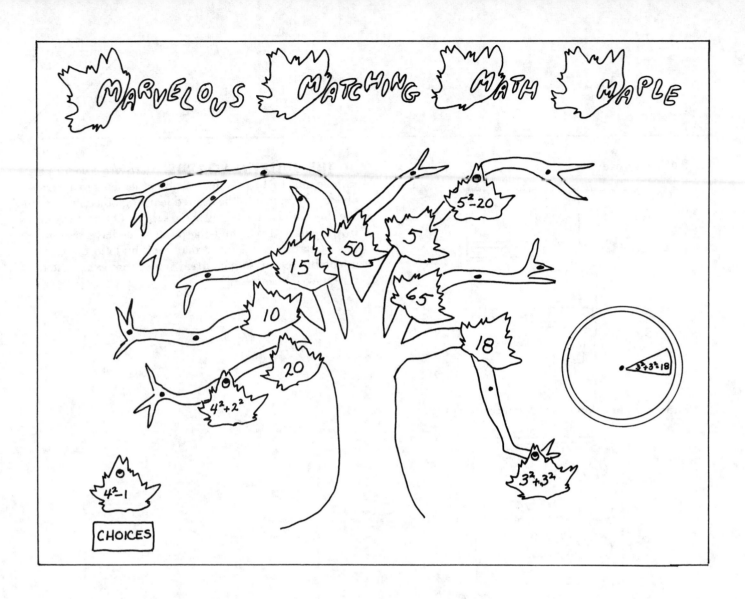

1 ▶ MARVELOUS MATCHING MATH MAPLE

SUBJECT   Mathematics.

OBJECTIVE   To use knowledge of exponents to match equivalent expressions.

CHALLENGE   *1 Match-Up.*

ASSEMBLIES   *1 Pockets and Slots, 3 Hooks and Pushpins, or 6 Pinch-On Clothespins.* Cut at least ten leaves, each to contain half of an equivalent expression.

THEME   A maple tree with leaves of colors suited to the season.

ANSWERS   *7 Turning Dials.*

RECORDS   None.

ACTIVITY   Each tree branch has a permanent leaf that carries one half of an equivalent expression. Students make matches by attaching leaves bearing the other half of the expression. (A leaf reading $10^2 - 90$ is correctly placed on a branch with a permanent leaf reading 10.) When all the leaves are in place, dial the answers.

VARIATIONS
1.   Change the matches periodically. Change the leaves to match the seasons (use snowflakes in winter).
2.   For social sciences, each branch can name a continent, with countries printed on the leaves. Change the caption to *Marvelous Mapping Maple.*
3.   For science, each branch can name a habitat, with the leaves containing names of animals living in each habitat. Change the caption to *Animal Tree House.*

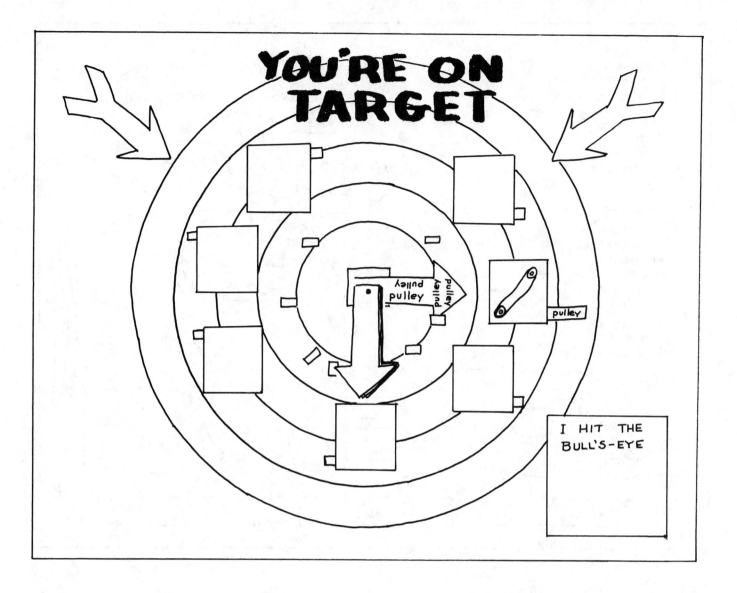

2 ► YOU'RE ON TARGET

SUBJECT Science.

OBJECTIVE To identify simple machines.

CHALLENGE *1 Match-Up.*

ASSEMBLY *12 Circling Arrows.*

THEME Archery targets.

ANSWERS *4 Pull Tabs.*

RECORDS *1 Autograph Sheet*, titled "I Hit the Bull's-eye!"

ACTIVITY Students rotate arrows until they match the picture of a simple machine with its name. They pull tabs to check answers.

VARIATION Change the pictures and vocabulary to suit the subject matter being taught.

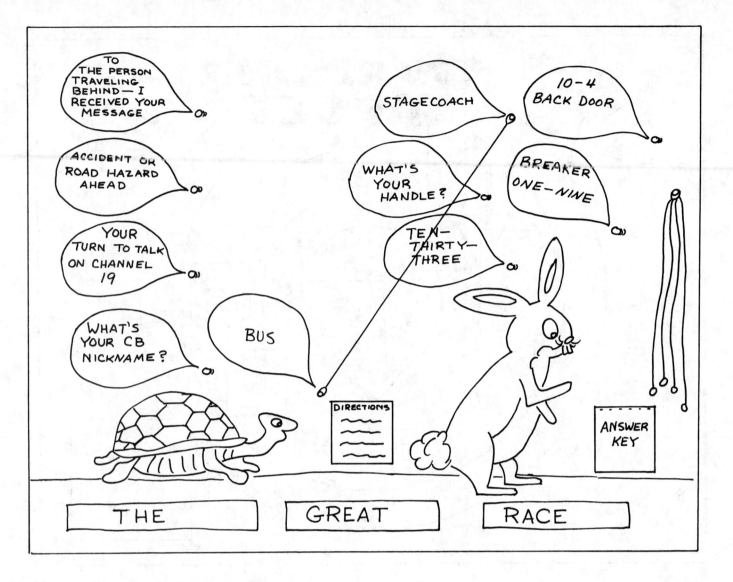

3 ► THE GREAT RACE

SUBJECT Language arts.

OBJECTIVE To become familiar with the different types of language—slang, formal, and specialized—through the interpretation of citizen's band (CB) slang.

CHALLENGE *1 Match-Up.*

ASSEMBLY *4 Strings Alone.*

THEME The race between the tortoise and the hare.

ANSWERS *1 Flaps.*

RECORDS None.

ACTIVITY Cartoon balloons contain CB expressions. The students match these expressions with cards containing the standard English forms.

VARIATIONS
1. Cartoon balloons contain figurative language expressions to be matched to the standard English forms.
2. Cartoon balloons contain abbreviations, with the entire word on the matching card.
3. Use foreign language expressions and their English equivalents.

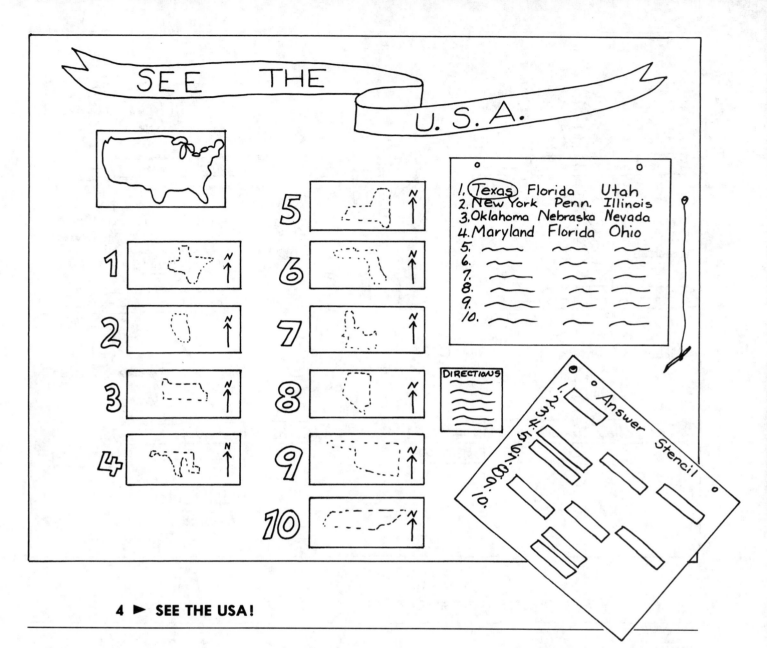

4 ► SEE THE USA!

SUBJECT Social science.

OBJECTIVE To identify states by their shapes.

CHALLENGE *1 Match-Up.*

ASSEMBLIES *15 Wipe-Offs* and *16 Touch and Tell.* You will need a map of the United States.

THEME A trip across the United States.

ANSWERS *5 Stencil.*

RECORDS None.

ACTIVITY Touch-and-tell cards hide the shapes of the states. The wipe-off card contains the choices. Students feel each shape through the fabric and circle their choices on the wipe-off card. Answers are checked using a stencil.

VARIATIONS

1. Use the shapes of countries. Change the caption to "Where in the World Are You?"

2. Add challenge *4 Sort Out.* After the shape of each country or state is identified it must be placed in the correct continent or in its correct position in the United States.

Robert Wadlow

1. The tallest man is ☐ [8 ft. 1 in.]

Howard Libbey Redwood

2. The tallest tree is ☐ [317 ft.]

Mount Everest

3. The tallest mountain is ☐ [29,002 ft.]

Answers

Ginny Bunford

4. The tallest woman is ☐ [7 ft. 7 in.]

Sears Tower

5. The tallest building is ☐ [1454 ft.]

Angel Falls

6. The tallest waterfall is ☐ [3,212 ft.]

Choices

5 ► GUINNESS GOES METRIC

SUBJECT Mathematics.

OBJECTIVE To estimate metric equivalents for English measures.

CHALLENGE *1 Match-Up.*

ASSEMBLY *1 Pockets and Slots.*

THEME *Guinness Book of World Records.*

ANSWERS *7 Turning Dials.*

RECORDS None.

ACTIVITY Students read the English measure and select the best equivalent for it, placing the cards in the correct slots.

VARIATIONS

1. Vary the units of measure to include units of volume and weight.
2. Simply have the children choose the best measure for each item.
3. Calculating may be practiced by providing several choices for each item—one exact and one close.
4. Tie the board to using an index. Students use the *Guinness* index to find the names of the tallest mountain, longest river, most venomous snake, and so on. Use a picture of the item, or just make a rough drawing.
5. To extend vocabularies, provide slots to hold word cards that describe the Guinness record-holder. ("Tallest" becomes "most formidable" and "smallest" becomes "most diminutive" or "puniest.")

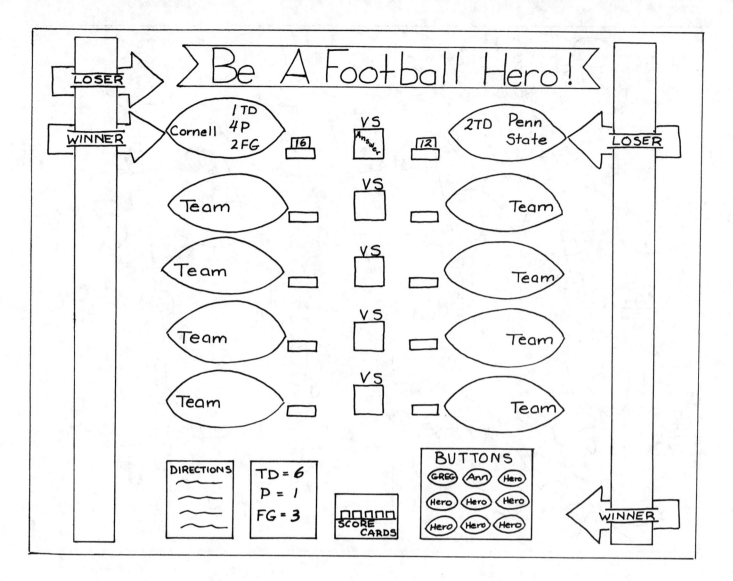

6 ► BE A FOOTBALL HERO

SUBJECT Mathematics.

OBJECTIVE To practice adding and multiplying mentally.

CHALLENGES *1 Match-Up* and *6 Order It*.

ASSEMBLIES *1 Pockets and Slots* and *5 Sliding Arrows*.

THEME Football.

ANSWERS *1 Flaps*.

RECORDS *5 Buttons* (with buttons shaped like footballs).

ACTIVITY Working on one "game" at a time, students mentally compute score for each team and place exact score cards in the slots. The arrows are moved to indicate the winner and loser for that particular game. After checking the answer flap, students go on to the next game.

VARIATIONS
1. Use basketball as a theme, giving two points for a field goal and one point for a free throw. The National Basketball Association is trying a three-point field goal for baskets outside a 22-foot semicircle. Use this extra scoring feature to increase the difficulty.
2. Supply the win-loss records for each team and ask more advanced students for the winning percentages.

7 ► FISHING FOR WORDS

SUBJECT Language arts.

OBJECTIVE To review word attack skills.

CHALLENGE *1 Match-Up.*

ASSEMBLY *1 Pockets and Slots.*

THEME Fishing.

ANSWERS *1 Flaps.*

RECORDS None.

ACTIVITY Students take word cards shaped like fish from the storage pocket and put them on the correct hook.

VARIATIONS
1. More cards and slots can be provided so more than one fish will be caught on a given hook. Change the cards as the children are exposed to new vocabulary.
2. To work on mathematics, the fishers can be catching short word problems that can be solved by adding, subtracting, or multiplying. Change the caption.
3. The fishers can be catching correct interpretations of idiomatic expressions. Write the correct interpretations on the fish, changing the caption to fit.

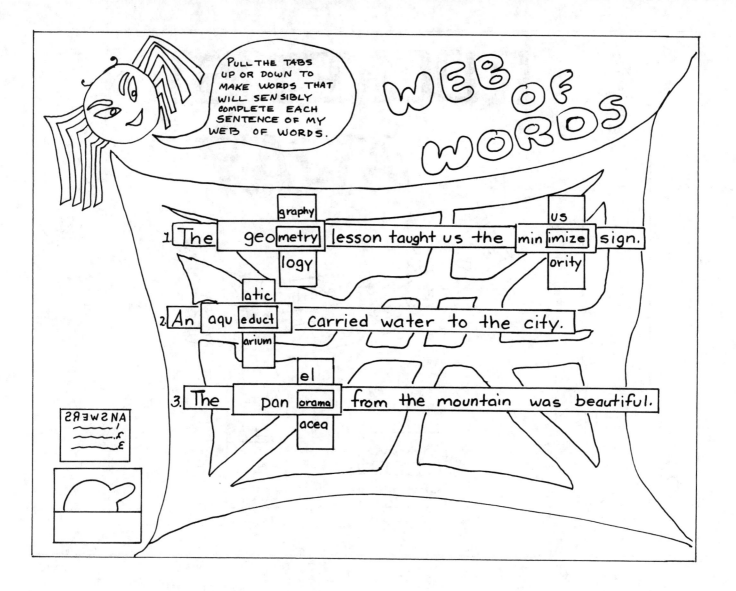

8 ► WEB OF WORDS

SUBJECT Language arts.

OBJECTIVE To choose the correct endings to complete sentences.

CHALLENGE *2 Fill in the Blanks.*

ASSEMBLY *13 Sliding Parts.* (Write the sentence on long strips, for easy changing, storage, and reuse.)

THEME A spider's web, suggesting that a sentence is also a web into which words must fit.

ANSWERS *2 Mirror Image.*

RECORDS None.

ACTIVITY The students pull the sliding part to complete the word and fit the context.

VARIATIONS
1. Use the sliding parts to improve spelling skills on easily confused words. Write *th* on the stationary part, and *eir*, *ey're*, and *ere* on the sliding part.
2. Change the caption and review math skills. The sliding parts can complete equations, or present definitions of terms or solutions to word problems.

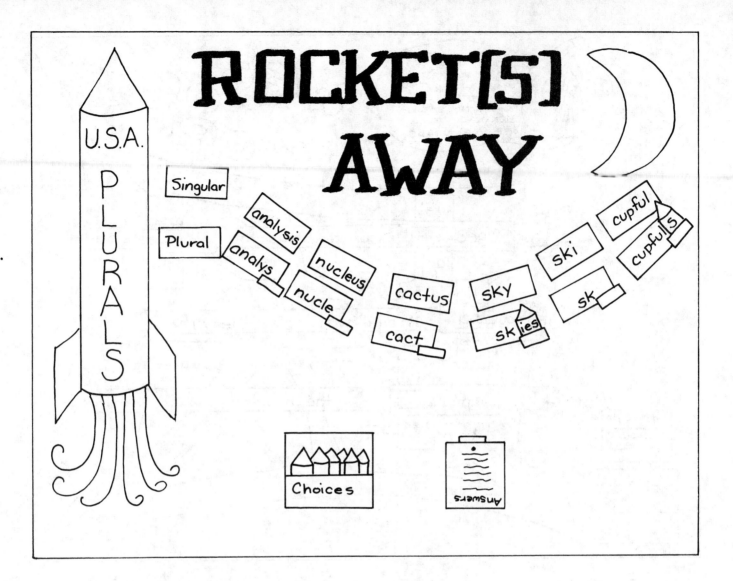

9 ► ROCKETS AWAY

SUBJECT   Language arts.

OBJECTIVE   To review rules for forming plurals.

CHALLENGE   *2 Fill in the Blanks.*

ASSEMBLY   *1 Pockets and Slots.* The slots are stapled under the word cards so that the letters placed in them can make the words plural.

THEME   Rockets and space.

ANSWERS   *3 Upside Down.*

RECORDS   None.

ACTIVITY   Students must place the letters to form plurals correctly. Then they check the answer key.

VARIATIONS

1. To reinforce verb tenses, provide letters that will form the past tense.
2. To review the use of prefixes that mean *not*, provide words which use the prefixes *un-*, *mis-*, *in-*, and so on.
3. Build words by adding prefixes and suffixes (*respect* becomes *disrespectfully*).
4. To work on mathematics, give equations with missing parts: 5 + 2 + ____ = 3 + 17.

10 ▶ JUGGLING ACT

SUBJECT   Mathematics.

OBJECTIVE   To use "greater than" and "less than" correctly.

CHALLENGE   *2 Fill in the Blanks.*

ASSEMBLIES   *1 Pockets and Slots* or *3 Hooks and Pushpins.*

THEME   Juggling act.

ANSWERS   *3 Upside Down.*

RECORDS   *1 Autograph Sheet.*

ACTIVITY   Each ball the juggler is using contains a pair of numbers with a slot or pushpin between them to hold a "greater than" or "less than" symbol. Students place the correct symbol in the slot or on the pushpin.

VARIATIONS
1. Increase the difficulty of the expressions.
2. Work on language arts. Use words that have vowel combinations which are often confused: fr*ie*nd, v*ei*l, rel*ie*ve, th*ei*r, bel*ie*ve, dec*ei*ve, n*ei*ghbor, c*ei*ling, rec*ei*ve, p*ie*ce. Students complete the word by positioning the omitted letters.

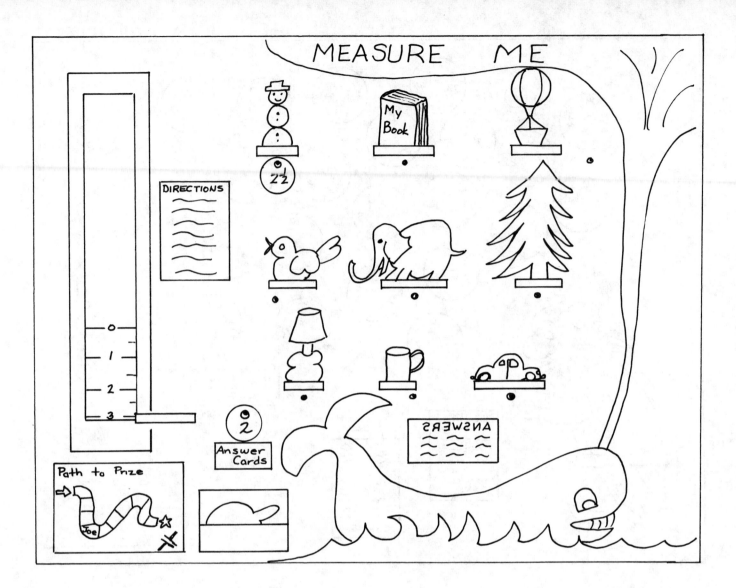

11 ► MEASURE ME

SUBJECT Mathematics.

OBJECTIVE To measure to the nearest centimeter.

CHALLENGE *2 Fill in the Blanks.*

ASSEMBLIES *3 Hooks and Pushpins* and *9 Watch It Grow.*

THEME The measuring machine.

ANSWERS *2 Mirror Image.*

RECORDS *4 Path to a Prize.*

ACTIVITY The object to be measured is removed from its hook or pushpin and placed in the slot next to the measuring machine. To operate the machine, the student slides the watch-it-grow roll to the place where the zero is aligned with the top of the item being measured, then reads the measurement at the baseline. The student then selects the appropriate measurement card and hangs it next to the object just measured.

VARIATIONS
1. Instead of providing objects with measurements very close to an exact number, supply objects which require interpolating to the nearest unit.
2. Provide a scale (1 cm = 1 m, for instance) and have the measurement converted from one unit to the other.
3. Provide shapes with a length and width, and have the student mentally compute areas or perimeters.

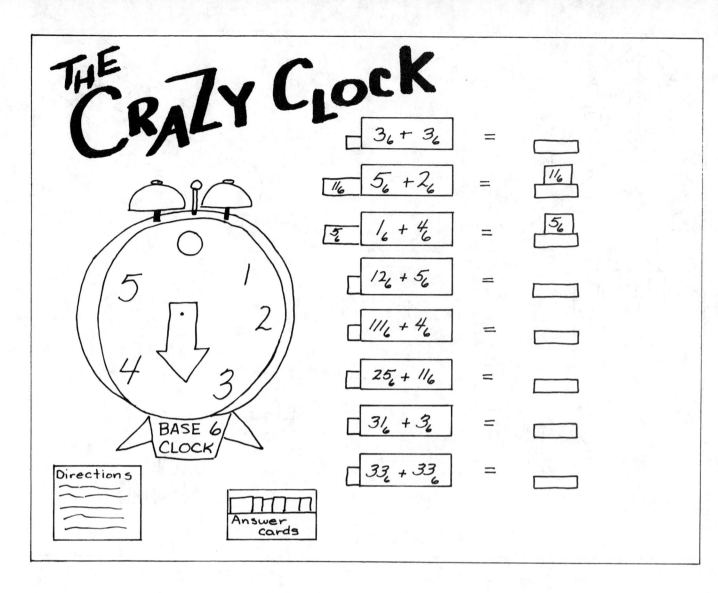

12 ► THE CRAZY CLOCK

SUBJECT   Mathematics.

OBJECTIVE   To use knowledge of different bases.

CHALLENGE   *2 Fill in the Blanks.*

ASSEMBLIES   *1 Pockets and Slots, 8 Turning Dials,* and *15 Wipe-Offs.*

THEME   Clocks and time.

ANSWERS   *4 Pull Tabs.*

RECORDS   None.

ACTIVITY   Students turn the dial the number of intervals needed to complete the equation, and place an answer card in the spot provided (or write the answer on the wipe-off equation card). Pull tabs reveal the correct answers.

VARIATIONS

1. Change the equation cards and dial according to the base studied.
2. Make a normal clock and allow the students to manipulate the hands to match statements you provide: "Time for recess," "One quarter-hour before lunch time," and so on.
3. To increase understanding of time changes across the United States or around the world, provide a suitable map and clock faces for each time zone. Students manipulate the clocks to answer questions: If it is 8 A.M. in New York City, what time is it in Paris, France?"

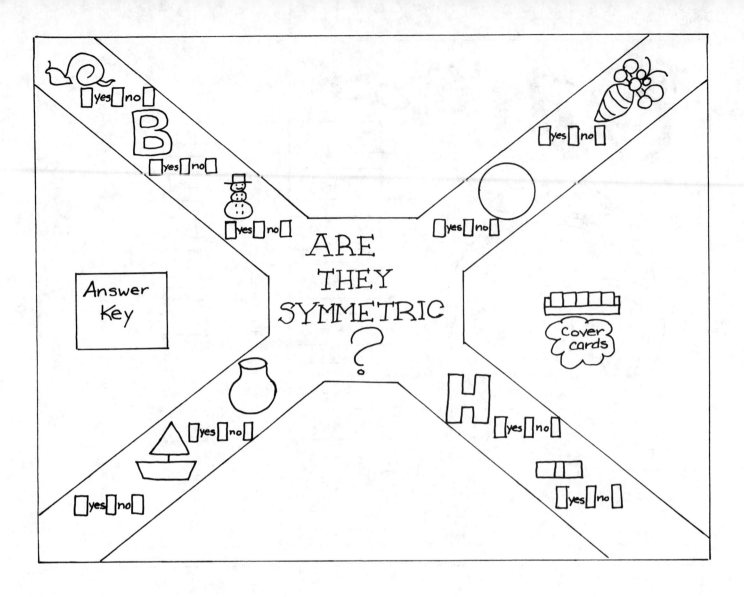

13 ► ARE THEY SYMMETRIC?

SUBJECT Mathematics.

OBJECTIVE To distinguish shapes that are symmetrical from shapes that are not.

CHALLENGE *3 Yes or No.*

ASSEMBLIES *7 Cover-Ups* and *1 Pockets and Slots.* Commercial or teacher-made pictures.

THEME Symmetry.

ANSWERS *1 Flaps.*

RECORDS None.

ACTIVITY Students examine the shapes and use cover cards to block the incorrect answers.

VARIATIONS
1. Check spatial perception by presenting a series of shapes with another series that is either identical or merely similar. Students decide if the sets are identical. Change the caption.
2. Use yes or no questions for a social studies or science bulletin board about food. Caption it *Are these meals balanced?* Use magazine cutouts to show the foods.

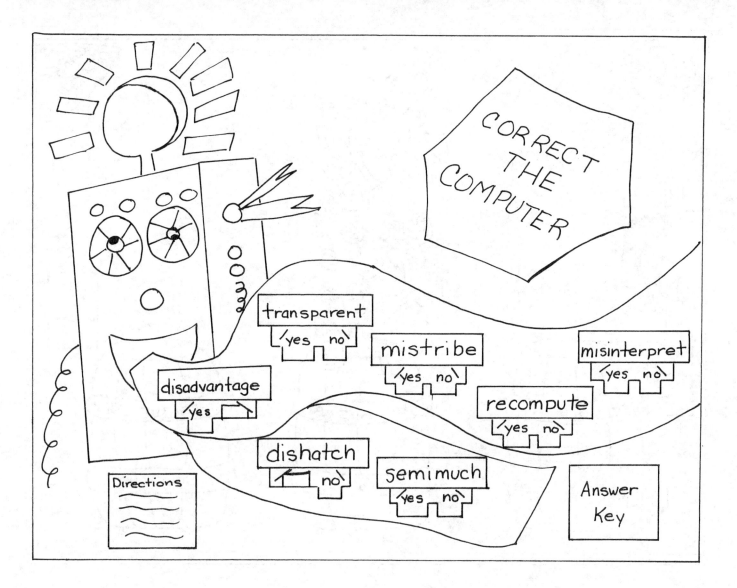

14 ► CORRECT THE COMPUTER

SUBJECT   Language arts.

OBJECTIVE   To review knowledge of affixes.

CHALLENGE   *3 Yes or No.*

ASSEMBLY   *10 Fold-Ups.*

THEME   Computers.

ANSWERS   *1 Flaps.*

RECORDS   None.

ACTIVITY   Students look at the words provided by the computer and, using a dictionary, cover the incorrect answers.

VARIATIONS

1. Make several sets of words and change them periodically.
2. To check for pronunciation, set up a basic question: "Do these words have a long *o* sound?" The computer output could be *plateau, notion, elbow, ocelot,* and *bough.*
3. Use social studies or science to suggest the basic question: "Are these part of a plant cell?" The computer output could be: *cell wall, tissue, cytoplasm, chloroplast, elodea,* and *ligament.*
4. Math is a natural subject for a computer: "Do these expressions name 1000?" (10^2, $9999 + 1$, $1211 - 221$, ½ of 20000, 10^3, 50% of 2000, $888 + 112$)

15 ► A BARREL OF MONKEYS

SUBJECT Mathematics.

OBJECTIVE To review the divisibility rules for 2 and 3.

CHALLENGE *4 Sort Out.*

ASSEMBLIES *1 Pockets and Slots* and *3 Hooks and Push-pins.* Teacher-made cards.

THEME Monkeys.

ANSWERS *1 Flaps.*

RECORDS None.

ACTIVITY Students take a monkey number from the choices and hang it above the correct barrel.

VARIATIONS
1. Sort equivalent fractions.
2. Sort equations.
3. Sort division problems by estimating the quotients.
4. For science, sort parts of the systems of the body (respiratory, digestive, nervous, and circulatory).
5. In studying geography, sort monkeys into barrels labeled Cities, Nations, and States.
6. To develop a time perspective, sort inventions into barrels labeled "Between 1700 and 1799," "Between 1800 and 1899," and "Between 1900 and (the current year)." Small pictures of the inventions can be pasted on the monkeys.

16 ► FILL THE HOPPERS

SUBJECT Language arts.

OBJECTIVE To use vowel sounds to categorize words.

CHALLENGE *4 Sort Out.*

ASSEMBLY *1 Pockets and Slots.* Teacher-made word cards.

THEME Kangaroo.

ANSWERS *4 Pull Tabs.*

RECORDS None.

ACTIVITY Students take kangaroo-baby cards from the choice pocket and put them in the labeled kangaroo pouches. When finished, they review their work by checking the pull-tab answer key.

VARIATIONS
1. Sort words by the number of syllables.
2. Sort words by the accented syllable.
3. Sort words by rules (for adding suffixes: drop the silent *e*, double the final consonant, or make no changes).
4. Sort adjectives into categories to promote the use of more vivid modifiers: big, small, pretty, and ugly.

17 ► SENTENCE MAGIC

SUBJECT Language arts.

OBJECTIVE To construct declarative, interrogative, imperative, and exclamatory sentences.

CHALLENGE 5 *Arrange Parts.*

ASSEMBLY 1 *Pockets and Slots.* Teacher-made word cards.

THEME Magic.

ANSWERS 4 *Pull Tabs.*

RECORDS None.

ACTIVITY There is a different color card pack for each hat, but each pack contains the same words and punctuation. Students construct the kind of sentence suggested by the rabbit. Not all cards will be used for each sentence. Answers are checked by pulling the tab next to the hat.

VARIATIONS
1. Definitions are held by the rabbits. The magic packs contain synonyms or antonyms.
2. Each rabbit holds a present tense sentence. Each sentence must be transformed to a different tense.
3. Use math rabbits, each holding a number. The magic pack contains numbers and operation symbols. An equation must be made to equal the rabbit's number.

18 ► PAVING THE WAY

SUBJECT Mathematics.

OBJECTIVE To practice mental addition.

CHALLENGE *5 Arrange Parts.*

ASSEMBLY *8 Turning Dials.*

THEME Street paving.

ANSWERS *1 Flaps.*

RECORDS None.

ACTIVITY Students turn the dials to produce as many combinations as possible that equal the given sum.

VARIATIONS
1. As the ability of your group changes, increase the difficulty of the addition.
2. Use subtraction, multiplication, or division.
3. For language arts, use compound words with definitions (passenger car is an auto-mobile).

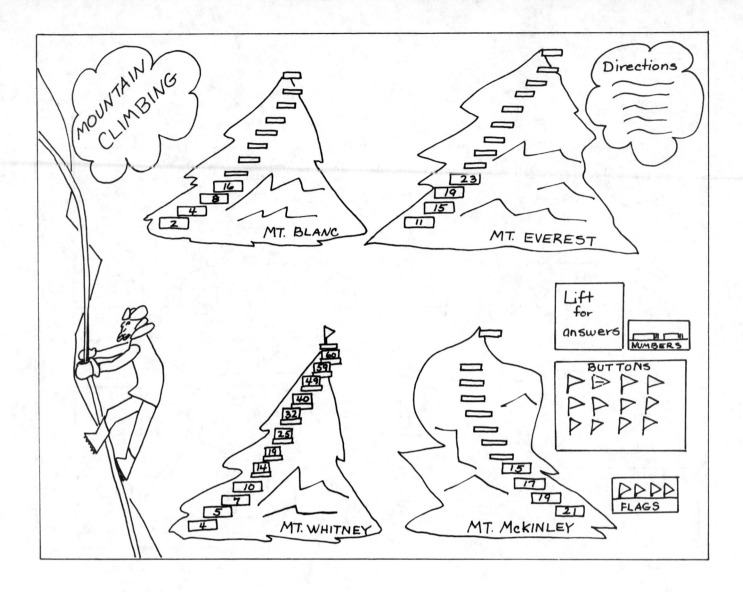

19 ► MOUNTAIN CLIMBING

SUBJECT Mathematics.

OBJECTIVE To determine number sequences or patterns and then extend them.

CHALLENGE *6 Order It.*

ASSEMBLY *1 Pocket and Slots.* Teacher-made number cards.

THEME Mountain climbing.

ANSWERS *1 Flaps.*

RECORDS *5 Buttons.* Make flags to be awarded to all who reach each summit.

ACTIVITY Students analyze each sequence and use the number cards to continue the pattern. When they reach the summit they place a flag in the slot. After checking, each receives a flag button.

VARIATIONS
1. Construct one giant mountain with several pathways. Students try to be first to reach the top.
2. Challenge *6 Order It* presented several types of sequences. Choose a science topic for sequencing, such as the path of sound through the ear, the digestive process, the water cycle, or food chains.

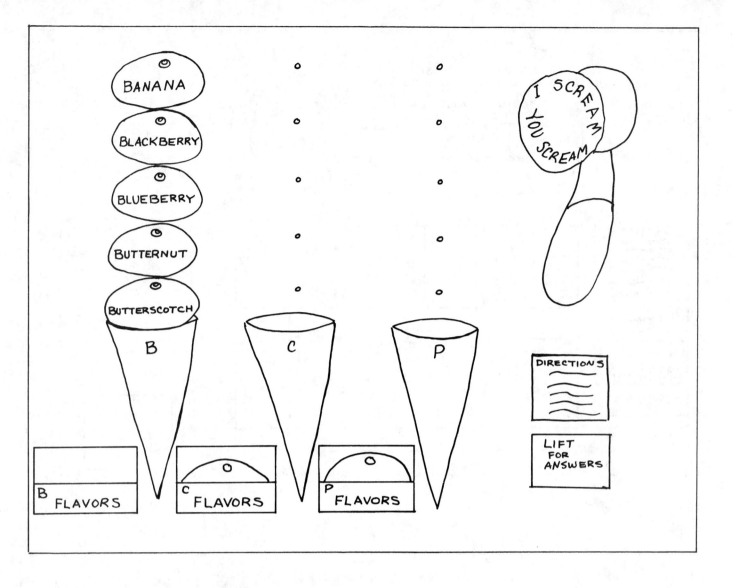

20 ► I SCREAM YOU SCREAM

SUBJECT Language arts.

OBJECTIVE To use alphabetizing skills.

CHALLENGE *6 Order It.*

ASSEMBLIES *1 Pockets and Slots* and *3 Hooks and Push-pins.* Teacher-made ice-cream scoop word cards.

THEME Ice cream.

ANSWERS *1 Flaps.*

RECORDS None.

ACTIVITY Students place the scoops in alphabetical order from top to bottom, then check the answer key.

VARIATIONS Use ideas in any subject area that lend themselves to sequencing: stops on trip across the country, steps in planting a garden, steps in building a soap-box racer, and so on.

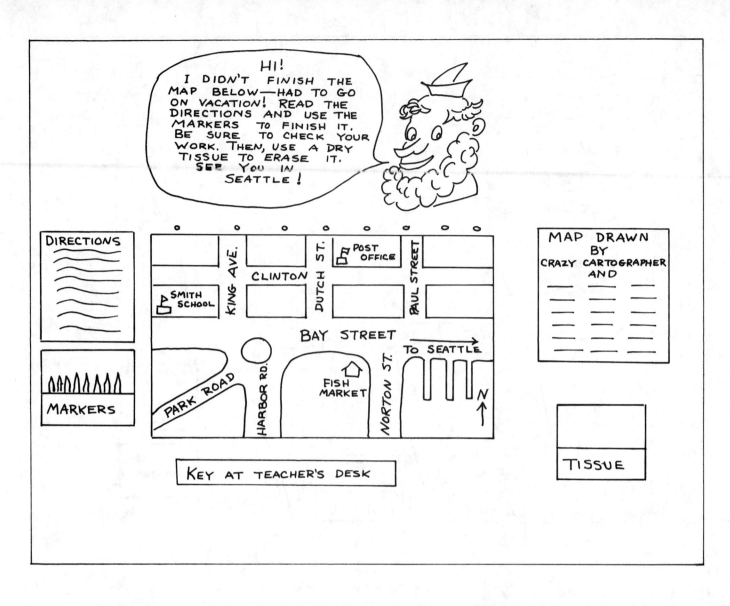

21 ► THE CRAZY CARTOGRAPHER

SUBJECT   Social science.

OBJECTIVE   To use map-reading skills.

CHALLENGE   7 *Write-It.*

ASSEMBLIES   *1 Pockets and Slots* and *15 Wipe-Offs.*

THEME   Street map, real or imaginary.

ANSWERS   *6 Overlays.*

RECORDS   *1 Autograph Sheet.*

ACTIVITY   Using washable markers, students follow directions: "Draw an arrow to show a bus route on Bay Street, traveling west." "Use a square to show a store on the southwest corner of the intersection of Clinton Street and King Avenue." Directions may be posted on a sheet of paper or printed on cards. After checking with the answer overlay, students wipe off their work.

VARIATION   Any diagram can be labeled. Science or social science topics include the parts of a flower, the parts of the eye or ear, geographical features, the parts of an electrical circuit, and states or countries.

GIFTS GALORE

	BIKE	GAME	CLOTHES	BOOKS
23				
22				
21				
20				
19				
18				
17				
16				
15				
14				
13				
12				
11				
10				
9				
8				
7				
6				
5				
4				
3				
2				
1				
	BLUE	RED	YELLOW	GREEN

DIRECTIONS

MARKERS

HAPPY BIRTHDAY

---

22 ▶ GIFTS GALORE

SUBJECT Mathematics.

OBJECTIVE To participate in the development of a bar graph.

CHALLENGE 7 Write It.

ASSEMBLY 1 Pockets and Slots.

THEME Birthday gifts.

ANSWERS Built into the activity.

RECORDS None.

ACTIVITY Students pick their favorite birthday gift from those offered and color in the lowest space under that gift, using the suggested color. With a contrasting color, they sign their names in the blocks. (Use washable markers or crayons if the board will be reused.) Interpret the results in a group discussion.

VARIATIONS

1. Change the theme and caption. Graph the most popular movies, or the favorite TV shows, sports, foods, or books.

2. When teaching averages, plot test-score averages for a month. Students do the computations with teacher-supplied scores. An added bonus here is the incentive to improve the test scores.

3. Relate graphing to science study. Prepare a line-graph chart to record temperature or relative humidity or some other daily variable. Assign a student to make each day's recording.

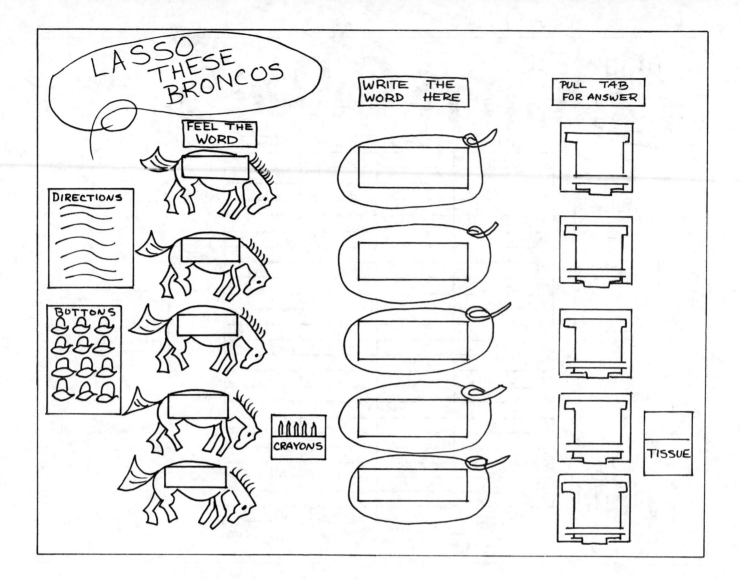

23 ► LASSO THESE BRONCOS

SUBJECT Reading.

OBJECTIVE To review reading vocabulary.

CHALLENGE *7 Write It.*

ASSEMBLIES *1 Pockets and Slots, 15 Wipe-Offs,* and *16 Touch and Tell.*

THEME Cowboys.

ANSWERS *4 Pull Tabs.*

RECORDS *5 Buttons,* made in the shape of ten-gallon hats.

ACTIVITY Students feel the touch-and-tell cards on the broncos to recognize reading words and use a crayon to record the words on the clear vinyl-covered cards in the lassos. Answers are checked by pulling the tabs.

VARIATIONS
1. Students can write their answers on paper which is then placed in an answers pocket.
2. The words identified on the board may be written in sentences to be handed in.
3. For math or art review, conceal numbers or shapes on the touch-and-tell cards.

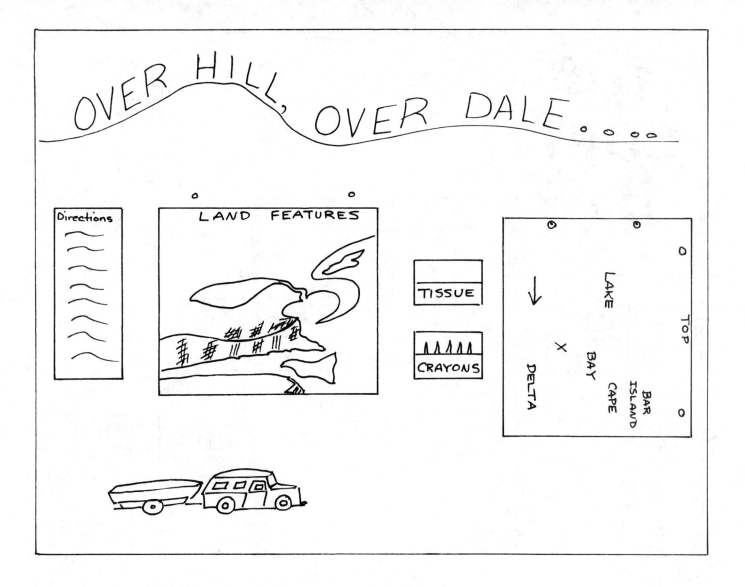

24 ► OVER HILL, OVER DALE

SUBJECT Social science.

OBJECTIVE To identify geographic features.

CHALLENGE *7 Write It.*

ASSEMBLY *15 Wipe-Offs.*

THEME All-terrain vehicles.

ANSWERS *6 Overlays.*

RECORDS None.

ACTIVITY Using the supplied list, students identify and write the names of the land features on the wipe-off map. The overlay provides a quick check.

VARIATIONS
1. Natural resources or products can be recorded on a wipe-off map.
2. States, countries, mountains, and bodies of water can be recorded.

25 ► COPY CAT

SUBJECT Mathematics, art.

OBJECTIVE To show perception of detail and spatial relationships by duplicating a design.

CHALLENGE *8 Copy It.*

ASSEMBLIES *3 Hooks and Pushpins* and *14 Tear-Offs.* Use grocery bags for instant pockets.

THEME Copy cat.

ANSWERS *6 Overlays,* or an answers pocket for teacher checking.

RECORDS None.

ACTIVITY Wearing the copy cat hat, the student selects a card to copy from the copy bag. The card is hung on a pushpin while being copied. Using the paper and writing materials supplied, the student copies the design. The copy is then checked with an overlay, torn off and placed in the finished copy bag to be checked by the teacher.

INSTRUCTIONS FOR COPY CAT HAT

SPECIAL MATERIALS Small grocery bags
Construction paper

PROCEDURE

1. Fold the bottom of the bag outward at the end and inward triangularly at the sides. Staple the closed folded end so that it lies flat.

2. Fold the open end over itself to make a hatband. Write "I'm a Copy Cat" on the hat as shown.

3. Cut ears from construction paper and staple them to the top of the hat.

4. Punch a hole at the top of the hat and hang it from a pushpin on the board.

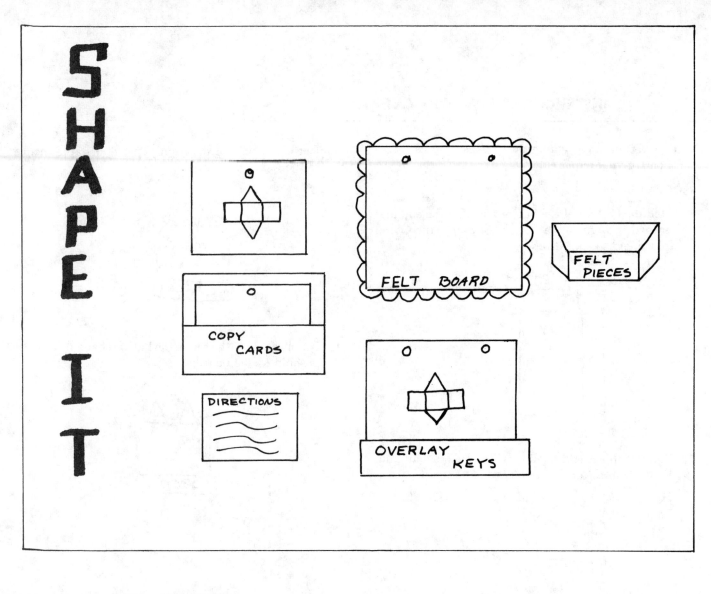

S H A P E   I T

26 ▶ SHAPE IT

SUBJECT Mathematics, art.

OBJECTIVE To copy a design.

CHALLENGE *8 Copy It.*

ASSEMBLIES *1 Pockets and Slots, 2 Felt Stick-Ons,* and *3 Hooks and Pushpins.*

THEME Geometric shapes.

ANSWERS *6 Overlays.*

RECORDS *6 Building Blocks,* or *7 Mystery Picture,* or a ditto score sheet.

ACTIVITY Students select a numbered copy card and hang it on the pushpin for copying. Felt pieces are selected from the supply and arranged in the copy card pattern. Overlays are used for checking.

VARIATION Use a tape recorder to give directions for making a design: "Place the largest orange triangle in the center of the board. Place one small red triangle on each corner of the board," and so on.

If most of your bulletin boards are now in action, those wide open spaces you used to wonder how you would fill are all in use. You may need added display areas for showing off those good papers and projects. Here are ten suggestions for stretching your display areas.

1 ► CLOTHESLINE

Clothesline can be stretched across areas of your room. Run the lines along the walls rather than across open space if your students are likely to see the lines as a challenge for jumping.

MATERIALS   Clothesline or strong twine
Clothespins or paper clips
Tools to anchor the lines

PROCEDURE
1. After asking yourself where the lines can be anchored easily and securely without becoming a temptation to jumpers, go ahead and anchor them firmly in place.
2. Prepare a Double Quick Caption (from Chapter 1).
3. Fasten the display material with clothespins or paper clips.

2 ► HANGER MOBILES

These mobiles can increase your display space attractively, cheaply, and quickly.

MATERIALS   Coat hangers
Masking or electrical tape
Paper clips, clothespins, or stapler

PROCEDURE
1. Tape the handles of two hangers to the lower corners of another hanger.
2. Staple, paper clip, or clothespin papers to the hangers (in pairs, for balance).
3. Prepare a Double Quick Caption (see Chapter 1).
4. Hang it up. You can use as many of these as space allows.

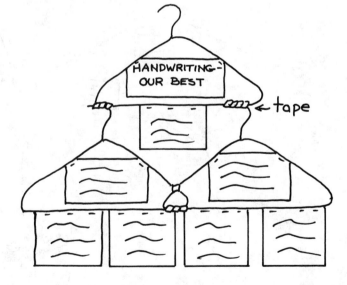

3 ► USE A TREE

Follow nature's example and use a tree!

MATERIALS   Tree branch
Wastebasket or bucket
Stones to fill bucket
Fasteners
Paper to cover bucket (optional)

PROCEDURE
1. *Optional*—cover the exterior of the bucket with kraft or other paper, leaving the handle free.
2. Prop the branch firmly in the bucket by filling the bucket with stones.
3. Prepare a Double Quick Caption (see Chapter 1).
4. Attach display materials with appropriate fasteners.

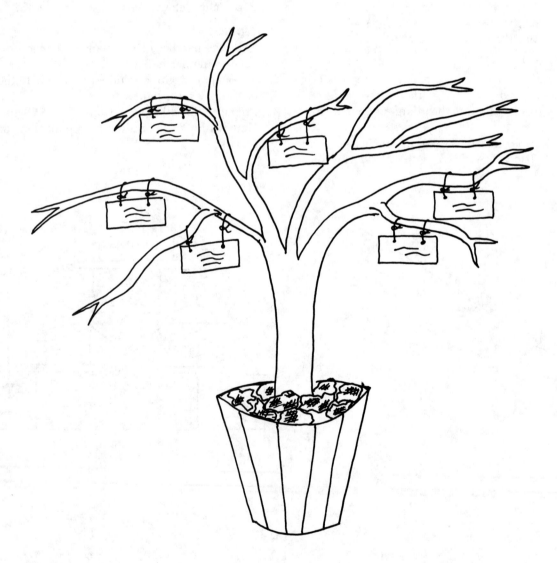

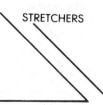

4 ▶ FLIP THE FLAPS

Use this method to display a lot of papers in a small area.

MATERIALS Tagboard or oaktag, 18" by 24"
Masking tape

PROCEDURE
1. Print a suitable title at the top of the tagboard.
2. Staple the display papers to the tagboard, beginning at the bottom, and adding papers as if you were shingling a roof. Try to allow each child's name to show.
3. Use masking tape or thumbtacks to anchor the tagboard to a flat surface.

5 ▶ DOORS ON DOORS

Construct a tagboard panel with paper doors. When the doors are opened, your message or the students' work is revealed. Post the panel on your classroom door.

MATERIALS Tagboard
Construction paper
Tools to anchor panel to classroom door

PROCEDURE
1. Staple student papers to both sides of construction-paper "doors," leaving one side of one door blank. This will be the top piece. Draw a picture of a door on it.
2. Starting at the righthand side, staple the doors to the tagboard so that they overlap. The last one to be stapled in place will be the one with the picture on the door. Staples should be along the left edge only, so that the doors will open and close.
3. Anchor the tagboard to your classroom door (or to a flat surface).

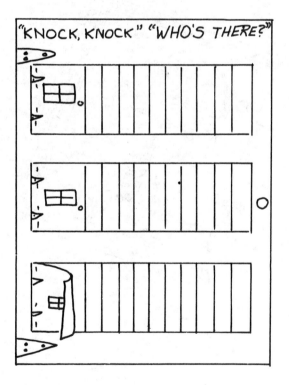

6 ► BOOKS

"Publishing" a book is an exciting class project and an efficient way to display work. A book is an excellent motivator for good handwriting and proofreading skills.

MATERIALS Cardboard or tagboard, 2 pieces
Paper clips, yarn, or string

PROCEDURE

1. Make the book cover by punching two matching holes near one edge of the tagboard pieces. Reinforce the underside of the holes with cellophane tape.
2. Print a title for the book on the top piece of tagboard.
3. Punch matching holes in all the student papers.
4. Open two paperclips in an S shape, or cut 25 cm (10 in.) pieces of yarn or string to fasten the cover and papers together.
5. Hook or tie the book together and put it on display.

7 ► ACCORDIONS

A quick display stand can be made from accordion-folded tagboard.

MATERIALS Tagboard or oaktag, 18" by 24" or larger
Tape, paper clips, or stapler

PROCEDURE

1. Using a meter stick and scissors, make an odd number of equally spaced vertical score lines on the tagboard. Score the first line on the front, the second on the back, the third on the front, and so on. Space the lines about 20 cm (8 in.) apart.
2. Fold on the score lines like an accordion.
3. Staple, paperclip, or tape the display work to the accordion. Use both sides.
4. Stand the accordion on a desk, table, or counter.

8 ► HANGING ACCORDIONS

An attractive display for vocabulary lists can be made by folding paper.

MATERIALS   Construction paper, 18" by 24"
Markers in three colors
Ruler

PROCEDURE

1. Prepare a list of eight words you wish to present—perhaps four synonyms and four antonyms.
2. Make twelve folds, forming thirteen spaces for writing. Each fold will be a little less than two inches apart.
3. In spaces 4, 7, and 10, respectively, use Color A marker to print "Learn These Words."

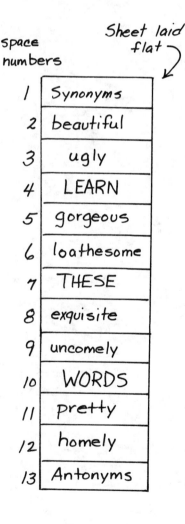

4. Use Color B marker to print "Synonyms" on space 1, and the synonym words in spaces 2, 5, 8, and 11.

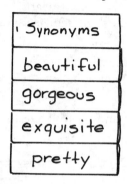

5. Use Color C marker to print "Antonyms" in space 13, and fill in the remaining spaces, 3, 6, 9, and 12, with antonyms.

6. Arrange folds as shown, to make four flaps, and staple or anchor on spaces 1, 4, 7, 10, and 13.

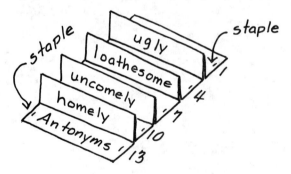

7. When the flaps are in a neutral position the student reads "Learn These Words." When the flaps are moved up, the antonyms appear, and when the flaps are moved down, the synonyms appear.

VARIATIONS   Use definitions for the slots printed in Color B, and print the meanings in Color C.

9 ▶ DISPLAY STANDS

Make a display rack for charts or students' papers (fastened to tagboard for showing off). Store the racks flat for reuse.

MATERIALS Cardboard or tagboard, at least 50 cm (20 in.) by 20 cm (8 in.)

PROCEDURE

1. Use the ruler and utility knife to cut out the area shown.

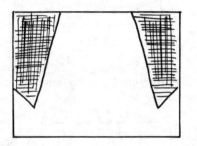

2. Make a vertical score in the center back and fold.

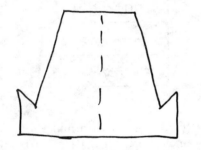

3. Stand the rack up and place the chart on it.

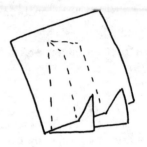

80

10 ► WINDOW ON MY WORLD

Students prepare their own windows and choose samples of their best work for display. It is illuminating to see the personal standards a child uses in making choices. You may wish to develop group standards for making display choices.

MATERIALS Construction paper, 18" by 24" for each student

PROCEDURE

1. Fold each piece of construction paper in half to make a 9" by 12" rectangle.

2. Use the ruler and scissors to cut out a frame on one side of the folded paper.

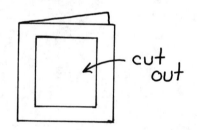

3. Staple the edge opposite the fold and the bottom edge, leaving the top open to slide the display papers in and out.

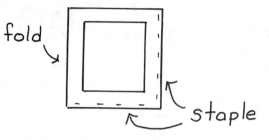

4. Slide student's papers in. The window can be attached to the student's desk or displayed elsewhere.

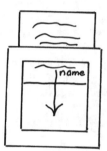

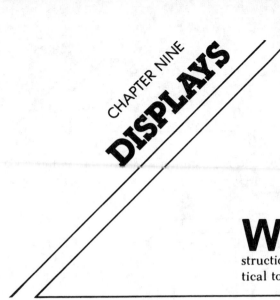

When you need to provide space for exhibiting realia of various kinds or to allow quick access to supplies, you can do so by using one of the five constructions that follow. When you are displaying delicate materials, it is often practical to use plastic wrap and cellophane tape to make protective coverings.

1 ► SHOE BOXES

Make small shelves from shoe boxes in order to display three-dimensional items on a board.

MATERIALS Shoe boxes (without tops)
Paper, *Con-Tact*®, or paint to cover boxes

PROCEDURE
1. Cut off and discard one long side from each shoe box.
2. Paint or cover each. Pick a light color for interiors.
3. Staple the remaining long side to the board to make a small shelf.

2 ► PYRAMIDS

Pile corrugated cardboard boxes in pyramid form for displaying or dispensing materials

MATERIALS Six cardboard boxes, equal in size (or three of one size, two smaller ones, and one still smaller for the top)
Paper, *Con-Tact*®, or paint to cover boxes

PROCEDURE
1. Remove the four flaps that close the boxes.
2. Cover with paper, or paint the exteriors. Paint the interiors.
3. Stack the boxes to form a pyramid.

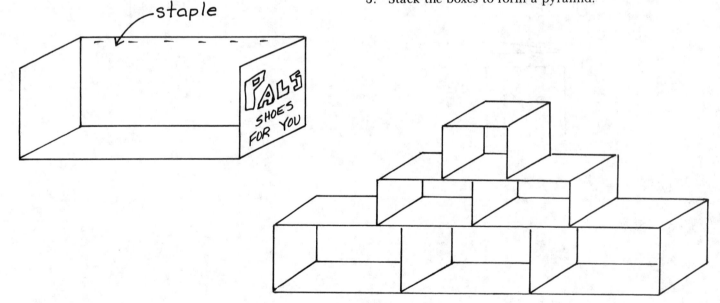

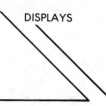

3 ► STAIRSTEPS

Staple boxes to a bulletin board in stairsteps and items can be placed on the steps as well as in the boxes.

MATERIALS   Boxes, same size
Paper, paint, or *Con-Tact*®

PROCEDURE
1. Remove the flaps from the boxes.
2. Cover with paper or paint.
3. Staple the boxes to the board in a stairstep pattern.

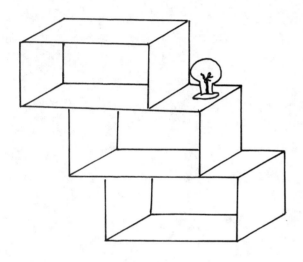

4 ► DIVIDERS

Use a beverage box with dividers for instant pigeon holes, or use the divider alone. You can use dividers to make a classroom post office for quick distribution of papers.

MATERIALS   Beverage box with dividers
Paper, *Con-Tact*®, or paint

PROCEDURE
1. Remove the flaps from the box.
2. Pull out the divider and cover the box.
3. Optional—take the divider apart and paint the pieces a light color.
4. Put the divider back in the box.
5. Make masking tape labels for names.

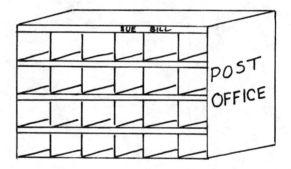

VARIATIONS
1. Use the divider alone by removing the bottom sections of the vertical dividers to make a flat base.
2. Remove portions of the dividers to increase the size of the pigeon holes.

5 ▶ DISPENSERS

For very simple dispensers, use *1 Pockets and Slots*, and attach them with tape to a door or cabinet. For more permanent dispensers, use cardboard and the following directions.

MATERIALS   Cardboard, or heavy tagboard
Construction paper
Paper, paint, or *Con-Tact®*

PROCEDURE

1. Make a pattern from construction paper, following the dimensions on the diagram. Trace the pattern on cardboard and cut it out (or measure and cut the cardboard without making a pattern).

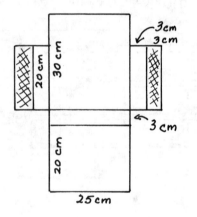

2. Glue, staple, or tape the flaps.

3. Cover the exterior if necessary.

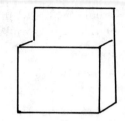

4. Stand or attach the dispenser in the desired location.

84

It is a great timesaver to store your bulletin board items carefully for future use. Begin your storage plans with a 3 by 5 file box; make a card for each board. On the card, note the objective, the theme, the date used, and where the materials are stored. File by objective, by unit of study, or by any other system that suits your needs. When you need a bulletin board, simply consult your file. For the materials themselves, you can use one or all of the following three methods.

1 ► BROWN BAG IT

Save your grocery bags and convert them into storage pockets.

MATERIALS   Grocery bags
Masking tape
Envelopes, standard size

PROCEDURE

1. Remove the bottom from a grocery bag.

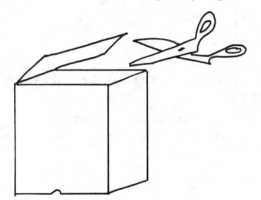

2. Flatten the bag and seal the bottom with masking tape, forming an envelope.

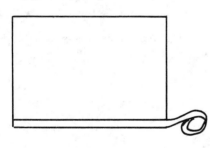

3. Fill out a file card.

4. Make a rough sketch of the bulletin board on the outside of the envelope. Include the caption.

5. Remove letters and store in a standard-size envelope. Print the caption on the outside.

6. Slide the caption envelope and other board materials into the grocery bag pocket.

7. If some items are too bulky to fit in the grocery bag envelope, note on the outside where you have stored them.

VARIATION   Use two grocery bags with the bottoms removed to make a giant-size storage pocket. Cut both bags open at the seams and place one on top of the other (or place them side by side). Seal the edges with masking tape and follow the preceding instructions.

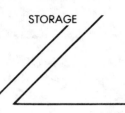

2 ▶ BOX IT

For large sheets, visit your local beverage dealer and acquire a beverage box with dividers. Label, roll, and place your materials in the sections. Be sure to note the location on the file card.

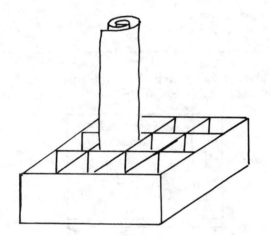

3 ▶ ENVELOPES

If you have no shelves for storing the grocery bag envelopes or you prefer a sturdier pocket, make envelopes from cardboard or oaktag.

MATERIALS Cardboard boxes, or oaktag
Masking tape
Envelopes, standard size

PROCEDURE

1. Remove top and bottom from the cardboard box.

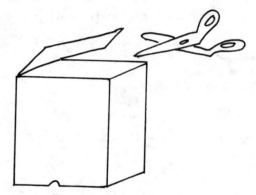

2. Flatten the box and seal the bottom edge with masking tape.

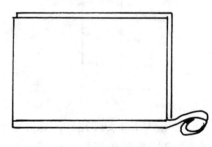

3. Follow the instructions for *1 Brown Bag It*.

VARIATION Use two large sheets of oaktag, sealed on three sides, to make a storage envelope.